Barnes & Noble Shakespeare

David Scott Kastan
Series Editor

BARNES & NOBLE SHAKESPEARE features newly edited texts of the plays prepared by the world's premiere Shakespeare scholars. Each edition provides new scholarship with an introduction, commentary, unusually full and informative notes, an account of the play as it would have been performed in Shakespeare's theaters, and an essay on how to read Shakespeare's language.

DAVID SCOTT KASTAN is the Old Dominion Foundation Professor in the Humanities at Columbia University and one of the world's leading authorities on Shakespeare.

Barnes & Noble Shakespeare
Published by Barnes & Noble
122 Fifth Avenue
New York, NY 10011
www.barnesandnoble.com/shakespeare

Image on p. 246:
William Shakespeare, *Comedies, Histories, & Tragedies*, London, 1623, Bequest of Stephen Whitney Phoenix, Rare Book & Manuscript Library, Columbia University.

Library of Congress Cataloging-in-Publication Data

Shakespeare, William, 1564–1616
  The tempest / [William Shakespeare].
    p. cm. — (Barnes and Noble Shakespeare)
  Includes bibliographical references.
  ISBN-13: 978-1-4114-0076-4 (alk. paper)
  ISBN-10: 1-4114-0076-3 (alk. paper)
    1. Fathers and daughters—Drama. 2. Political refugees—Drama. 3. Shipwreck victims—Drama. 4. Magicians—Drama. 5. Islands—Drama. 6. Spirits—Drama. I. Title. II. Series: Shakespeare, William, 1564–1616. Works. 2006.

PR2833.A1 2006
822.3'3—dc22

                                    2006009485

Printed and bound in the United States.
1 3 5 7 9 10 8 6 4 2

THE TEMPEST

William
SHAKESPEARE

GORDON McMULLAN
EDITOR

Barnes & Noble Shakespeare

Contents

Introduction to *The Tempest*
by Gordon McMullan

n 1623, purchasers of the Shakespeare First Folio found *The Tempest* in pride of place at the very beginning of the volume—an order that suggests that Heminge and Condell, friends and colleagues of the playwright who assembled his plays for publication seven years after his death, must have had a particular regard for what is now the best known of Shakespeare's last plays. *The Tempest* is unquestionably one of Shakespeare's finest achievements, one for which the dramatist gave himself at the same time tight strictures and endless possibilities, binding himself to the classical unities he ignores in his other late plays—so that the action of the play technically happens in one location, lasting only as long to perform as it takes for events to unfold in real time—yet freeing himself, like his spirit-character Ariel, to play fast and loose with geography and temporality. It is also a play—arguably more than any other in the Shakespeare canon—that makes sense fully only in performance, when its characters, earthy or ethereal, inhabit a weird soundscape of storms, disembodied songs, and eerie noises, and its audiences experience disorienting visuals: a shipwreck, a harpy, and a troupe of masquing goddesses. Mixing *realpolitik* with dreams, carnival insurrection with insubstantial pageant, *The Tempest* draws the audience into a story and a terrain that stays with them long after they have left the theater. It is Shakespeare's strangest play, its strangeness emerging from the tension between its outward urge and inward focus—its spatial expansiveness and emotional intensity—a tension that is characteristic of the genre to which it belongs and of which it is at the same time the most distilled example and the least characteristic.

Critics usually group *The Tempest* with three other plays in the Shakespeare canon, all written within five or so years toward the end of his career as chief playwright for the King's Men. These other plays are *Pericles* (now considered a collaboration with the minor playwright George Wilkins), *Cymbeline*, and *The Winter's Tale*, a group known as Shakespeare's late plays, romances, or—to use a cumbersome but perhaps more technically accurate term—romantic tragicomedies. Yet if the only point of access to these plays were still the 1623 Folio, they would not form an obvious group, spread as they are around the sections entitled "Comedies" and "Tragedies" (or, in the case of *Pericles*, which was published only in quarto form, not there at all). The urge to establish a shared generic identity for these plays postdates Shakespeare's day and offers only provisional answers. Neither *tragicomedy* nor *romance* fits comfortably, the one failing to evoke the mood of the plays, their embodiment of a sense of wonder, the other seeming to equate these innovative Jacobean dramatic texts with medieval prose narratives lacking both theatricality and currency. The coupling *romantic tragicomedy* overcomes some of the limitations of each of the separate terms, but still remains uncomfortably vague. None of these options, in other words, quite lives up to the full range of the play's possibilities, either in form or in theme. Its breadth of engagement with the physical space of the stage, with the flexibility of the actors on that stage, and with the audience's expectations means that it deserves better.

One alternative, the apparently neutral phrase *late play*, is often used as a means to avoid the problems of generic terminology, grouping the plays instead by way of chronology, but this, too, brings a certain amount of baggage. Since the middle of the nineteenth century, the *lateness* of *The Tempest* has been viewed as its main determining feature, reflecting the phase (it is claimed) that Shakespeare had reached in his own career. This produces readings that assume that a play's meaning emerges directly from the playwright's personal experience—even his mood at the time of writing—and it connects the Shakespearean "late plays" with the late work of other "great" writers, composers, or artists. For critic after critic—beginning with the Romantic poet and editor Thomas Campbell in the 1830s—Prospero and Shakespeare are one: when the mage, seeing the achievement of his life's work, finally gives up his art, breaking his staff and drowning his book, he is also Shakespeare, writing his last lines with a flourish before retiring, fulfilled, to Stratford. That characters are never the exact embodiment of their creator, that Prospero is perhaps a less saintly figure than we might prefer as a portrait of the aging Shakespeare, and that the facts are in any case simply wrong (we do not have any clear proof that *The Tempest* postdates *The Winter's Tale* or *Cymbeline*, whereas we do have evidence that he wrote three more plays collaboratively: *Henry VIII*, the lost *Cardenio*, and *The Two Noble Kinsmen*) have not daunted those determined to read the play in this way.

The Tempest has many more stories to tell than just this. It has, in fact, meant astonishingly different things to its audiences at different times. In 1970, to those watching Jonathan Miller's provocative production at the Mermaid Theatre, London, in which Ariel and Caliban became high- and low-caste natives respectively and Prospero the white colonial governor, it was a play of oppression and violence, uncomfortably redolent of the way in which postcolonial politics were playing themselves out across Africa. Miller had read Octave Mannoni's *Prospero and Caliban*, a controversial psychological analysis of colonialism that deployed *The Tempest* brilliantly as a metaphor for the relationship between colonist and colonized, and he found in the play the early origins of later struggles. Back in 1613, on the other hand, performed at court (two years after its first performance there) before an audience that included not only King James I but also his daughter Elizabeth and her new husband, Frederick, Elector Palatine, the play must have seemed resonant in quite different (though equally political) ways. The references in Act Two to the wedding of Alonso's daughter Claribel to the King of Tunis—with Alonso's lament that Claribel is now "so far from Italy removed / I ne'er again shall see her" echoed in the usurper Antonio's wry observation that she now "dwells / Ten leagues beyond man's life"—awkwardly address the conflicting emotions of a court overjoyed to see the young princess married to the principal Protestant ruler of a continent torn by sectarian violence but uncomfortably aware that she was about to cross the English Channel permanently to live in another country where her father's protection would be at best distant, at worst unavailable.

For a substantial period in the life of the play, however, these darker resonances from seventeenth or twentieth centuries were banished or simply unthinkable. The play was celebrated for its magical, imaginative qualities and its status as one of the very finest examples of a Shakespeare play (curious, then, that for over half of *The Tempest*'s performative life, it was Davenant and Dryden's 1667 adaptation and not Shakespeare's original that audiences saw at the theater). For the editor Nicholas Rowe, the play seemed "as perfect in its kind as almost anything we have of his." For the Romantics, *The Tempest*'s perfection lay in its detachment from history, its nature (in Coleridge's words) as a "birth of the imagination" owing "no allegiance to time or space," a play pure and simple, magical and rich. Ariel's song from late in Act One—

Full fathom five thy father lies.
Of his bones are coral made;
Those are pearls that were his eyes:
Nothing of him that doth fade
But doth suffer a sea-change
Into something rich and strange. (1.2.398–403)

offers the play's hallmark, expressing a transformative tendency that can turn hopelessness into renewal, violence into harmony. The island is such that even Caliban, the apparently reprobate aborigine and would-be rapist of Miranda, can rhapsodize about its "sounds and sweet airs" and show himself capable of dreams. The play's structure moves us steadily away from chaos and toward reconciliation, marriage, and general redemption. Prospero's plan is fulfilled, Miranda and Ferdinand are married, the royal houses of Milan and Naples are united, and social order—threatened with inversion both by the ambitions of the brothers, respectively, of a king and a duke and, briefly, by the comic rebellion of a butler and a clown—is reestablished. This, for many critics, makes the play essentially conservative, a paean to court culture that, by way of courtly forms such as the masque, demonstrates both the centrality of Prospero (and by implication King James I) to the establishment of cultural harmony and the play's generic function in confirming the intertwining of stability and hierarchy in a successful polity. And there is no doubt that the play follows to the letter the classic festive pattern, moving its audience from unease at social disharmony by way of delay and plot twist to relief at the reconciliation with which it concludes.

Yet for all that Ariel's song celebrates the magical, transformative potentialities of the island, the play is, as Stephen Orgel observes, "a story of privatives"—that is, of comforts and aspirations denied—"withdrawal, usurpation, banishment, becoming lost, shipwreck"—and it seems that no single character avoids loss, frustration, or displacement of some kind. This privation is, in a sense, structurally essential if the redemptive qualities of the island (and of the genre) are to be released: without loss, there can be no subsequent restoration. Even at the point at which Ferdinand learns that Prospero has set up his meeting with Miranda in order that they might marry, he receives a dire warning about his conduct prior to the wedding:

If thou dost break her virgin-knot before
All sanctimonious ceremonies may
With full and holy rite be ministered,
No sweet aspersion shall the heavens let fall
To make this contract grow, but barren hate,
Sour-eyed disdain, and discord shall bestrew
The union of your bed. (4.1.15–21)

Prospero's fears of the limitations of his power are obvious here: he may be able to control the weather, but he is afraid of human desire. His threats serve to remind us uncomfortably of Miranda's status as a pawn in a patriarchal exchange process: he has the entrenching of his dynasty in mind here, not his daughter's welfare. For her part, Miranda makes an apparently free choice of husband that is in fact dictated for her, and her amazement at the sight of the Neapolitan party at the end of the play—"O brave new world," she says, wide-eyed, "That has such people in 't!"—reminds us that she remains unaware both of the full extent of choice that has been denied her and of the function of marriage as social manipulation. Ariel's song offers the prospect of genuine metamorphosis, yet the play's concluding transformations seem hard pressed to override what we know of the preceding struggle—the anguish of exile, grief, and slavery. Unlike in the other late plays, the King's daughter Claribel, of whom we hear at the start but never meet, is never reunited with her father; and the years have visibly taken their toll on Prospero who, forgetting until it is almost too late the farcical rebellion of Caliban, Stephano, and Trinculo, needs to walk "a turn or two" to "still [his] beating mind" when he remembers. Ariel is freed at last from the threat of torture, of being again imprisoned in the "cloven pine," but there is no gratitude, only silence. And for too many of those on stage in the last scene— for Caliban, Sebastian, Antonio, Stephano, and Trinculo, and perhaps also for Miranda—the play's outcome is less than ideal.

The Tempest is peopled by as strange a bunch of characters as you will find in any of Shakespeare's plays: the one preexisting (though not indigenous) inhabitant of the island, enslaved and furious; a spirit of indeterminate gender whose suppressed resentment underpins a magical, musical lightness; an ineffectual king and a batch of royals and courtiers of various shapes and sizes, some of them vicious, at least one generous; an anarchic jester and a drunken butler; and an assortment of earthy sailors and insubstantial goddesses, nymphs, and reapers. Out of this curious and at times riotous assembly, Shakespeare molds a story that takes the Europeans outside their customary environment and gives them all a significance beyond their immediate function in the plot. In this context, it is in fact two of the most lightly drawn figures in the play who arguably best embody certain of the play's key qualities—one a minor character called Gonzalo who acts as a kind of effete royalist cheerleader when we first see him, the other a cruel witch called Sycorax who exists only in the memories and imaginations of the other characters.

Gonzalo is an apparently bumbling courtier who nonetheless manages to remain in favor with both usurper and usurped and who refuses to acknowledge the contradictions in the vision he conjures up of social perfection. His dramatic role is to force us to confront both the necessity and the futility of political dreams. His colonial vision, lifted near verbatim from an essay by Montaigne and heavily dependent on Thomas More's *Utopia*, suggests a genuine urge for liberty even as it projects a series of restrictions:

Had I plantation of this isle, . . .
. . . no kind of traffic
Would I admit. No name of magistrate.
Letters should not be known. Riches, poverty,
And use of service—none. . . .
All things in common nature should produce

Without sweat or endeavor. . . .
I would with such perfection govern, sir,
T' excel the Golden Age. (2.1.139–164)

Sebastian and Antonio underscore the elisions in his account as he
speaks, and we are left with a sense of genuine possibilities always
already fated to be impossibilities, because one person's freedom
is another's imprisonment. Nonetheless, Caliban elsewhere in the
play reminds us of what David Norbrook calls its "libertarian im-
pulse," its irrepressible desire for freedom—"Freedom, high-day,
freedom!" he chants—and, though we cannot help but agree with
Sebastian and Antonio's critique of Gonzalo's vision, his urge to
create a better way of life stays with us.

One feature of Gonzalo's speech mocked by Antonio and
Sebastian is his call for his commonwealth to be peopled with
"innocent and pure" women, the one notable addition to the material Shakespeare drew from Montaigne. It is the absent presence of
Caliban's mother Sycorax, however, which reminds us that women
are in fact mostly missing from *The Tempest*'s landscape. We hear
little of Prospero's wife, the echo of whose voice comes to us only in
her uncertain confirmation of Miranda's legitimacy; of Claribel, we
hear only that she has been sent to a faraway place to marry someone unwelcome. The one who remains—Miranda—is the most
malleable of her sex: young, eager, susceptible, as yet unmarried
but thoroughly (though she doesn't know it herself) marriageable,
she is both limited by her lack of social education and arguably just
plain spoiled. Sycorax, the "foul witch" who was Caliban's mother,
embodies everything Prospero (and perhaps the play) seems to fear
and reject in women. Originating in Algiers, the "damned witch,"
"blue-eyed hag," exiled because of her powers and pregnant with
a monster, arrived on the island and instantly set about coercing
Ariel to do her wishes, locking him in painful confinement when

he refused. This narrative makes it clear that Sycorax is Prospero's alter ego, a frightening female version of himself, just as Caliban is a disturbing male version of Miranda; her magic and his, represented as malign and benign respectively, seem in the end the same, leaving the magician-politician no choice but to reject his art in order to reestablish his civilized status.

It is Prospero who dominates *The Tempest*, a domination that, together with his magical abilities and the play's place in the Shakespeare chronology, has led, as I have noted, to an identification of character and playwright. The role of Prospero, along with that of King Lear, is one that Shakespearean actors of a certain stature—usually those who have played Hamlet in their youth—aspire toward the end of their career, the most obvious recent example being the casting of the aging Sir John Gielgud as a near-omnipotent mage in Peter Greenaway's film *Prospero's Books*, which carefully cuts the text of the play to de-emphasize the various ways in which Prospero's power is questioned. Yet, of course, the privative principle of the play operates also in Prospero. As with each of Shakespeare's last plays, the reconciliation—which invokes genuine wonder in cast and audience alike—comes at great cost, a cost counted in unclaimable years, wrinkles, and grief. Sixteen years is a long time to wait to reclaim your right, and the return home does not come without loss, as Prospero's exhaustion by the play's end and the obvious lack of remorse in his ice-cold brother Antonio both, in their different ways, make clear.

The human instincts to survive and to control are embodied in Prospero and Miranda, who use technology to control the indigenous population and reconstruct the alien environment of the island along familiar lines. At the other end of the scale of humanity, ostensibly, is Caliban. Yet by the end Prospero appears to admit kinship with, at least as much as ownership of, the play's visionary "cannibal" when he admits "This thing of darkness I / Acknowledge mine." Ariel inhabits a different sphere and flies away, but Prospero and Caliban remain locked in a relationship that neither of them desires. The humanity they share with their "slave" is, of course, deeply problematic for both Prospero and Miranda—the latter, with the intemperance of childhood, sees him as "filth," petulantly disappointed that she has failed to tame him with language—but it is inescapable. And as Paul Brown, Peter Hulme, and others argued in the 1980s, Caliban's anguished account of the process by which he has been transformed from sole inhabitant and thus ruler of the island to slave opens up a further, geopolitical dimension to the play:

> This island's mine, by Sycorax my mother,
> Which thou tak'st from me. When thou cam'st first,
> Thou strok'st me and made much of me, wouldst give me
> Water with berries in 't, and teach me how
> To name the bigger light and how the less,
> That burn by day and night. And then I loved thee
> And showed thee all the qualities o' th' isle:
> The fresh springs, brine pits, barren place and fertile.
>   Curs'd be I that did so! All the charms
> Of Sycorax—toads, beetles, bats—light on you,
> For I am all the subjects that you have,
> Which first was mine own king. And here you sty me
> In this hard rock, whiles you do keep from me
> The rest o' th' island. . . .
> You taught me language, and my profit on 't
> Is I know how to curse. (1.2.332–365)

In this poignant, furious narrative of displacement, cultures emerging from a history of colonization have heard the origins both of their own enslavement and of their urge for liberation, drawing on *The Tempest* for a rich tradition of postcolonial writing; equally, the former colonizing cultures have used the play, as the Miller production suggests, to exorcize their own awareness of the mistakes of the past and the ongoing impact of those mistakes.

The geography of _The Tempest_ has long been a source of debate and has provoked some of the finest criticism. It is no coincidence that, as the center of gravity in academic Shakespeare studies moved from Britain to the United States over the course of the twentieth century, _The Tempest_ became, as far as critical readings were concerned, an "American" play. Uniquely for one of Shakespeare's plays, nobody has been able to find a comprehensive source for _The Tempest_—for once, it seems, Shakespeare thought up the story by himself—but scholars have detected borrowings from a range of writers from Virgil to Montaigne. One source is a letter dated July 15, 1610, by a colonial venturer called William Strachey, describing his experiences on a ship journeying to relieve the Virginia plantation, that was shipwrecked on a Caribbean island (Caliban's name, a near-anagram of _cannibal_, also echoes the Caribs, a West Indian people). The play bears traces of this letter. Strachey's account of Saint Elmo's fire in the ship's rigging, for instance, is echoed closely in Ariel's claim to have "flamed amazement" about Alonso's ship before he tricked the voyagers into leaping into the sea. Add to this the spirit's reference to the "still-vexed Bermudas," along with Trinculo's mention of a "dead Indian" as a fairground attraction, and _The Tempest_ becomes a New World play, a play whose roots lie firmly in the early English colonization of America.

More recently, however, critics have begun to look more closely at the play's overt location not in the Caribbean at all, but in the Mediterranean somewhere off the coast of Tunis, thereby shifting the geographical focus of analyses of the play back toward the Old World. I have already noted the political significance for the early audiences of the marriage of Alonso's daughter Claribel and the king of Tunis, a dynastic arrangement echoed in the pairing of Alonso's son and Prospero's daughter, which itself echoes the alliances sought

by the Protestant James I in his quest to defuse the ongoing sectarian tensions in Europe. On the other hand, David Scott Kastan has
suggested that Prospero might have borne echoes for the first
audiences not of James I but of the Hapsburg ruler Rudolf II, the
Holy Roman Emperor (the most important Catholic leader other
than the Pope), who was notorious for having neglected state
business in favor of occult studies. These concurrent, mutually
resistant resonances underline the difficulty of reading Shakespeare's
plays in relation to the politics of his day, but whichever echoes
a member of the contemporary audience chose to hear, the play
shows clear signs of being at least as engaged with local European
concerns as with the far-off colonization of the New World.

Moreover, the general resonance of this play of sea changes
for a Europe geared to the technologies of maritime expansion has
prompted critics to see a further geographical orientation in *The
Tempest*'s Mediterranean setting, emphasizing its place at the point
of convergence between the cultures of Christianity and Islam in the
wake of the prolonged struggle in the preceding half century between
the Hapsburg and Ottoman Empires. Tunis, once Hapsburg controlled,
had for nearly a century been back in Muslim hands by the time
Shakespeare wrote his play. *The Tempest* negotiates these geopolitical
issues quietly by way, for instance, of the apparently meaningless
debates the characters have over the identity of Tunis and Carthage.
These debates invoke parallels between the classical world and the
world of Shakespeare's own day, as contemporary struggles between
Christian and Muslim for control over the sea that divided and
connected them are read as a rehearsal of ancient tensions between
Republican Rome and Carthage, her chief rival for empire. In this
way, Sycorax's malevolence, emerging from Muslim North Africa and
channeled by way of Caliban's violent tendencies, figures the threat
the Ottoman Empire posed to the European, Christian illusion of
being at the still center of the world, reading the rivalry between the

two cultures as a version of a near-apocalyptic political struggle of the classical past. The geography and temporality of *The Tempest* are, in other words, hybrid, and the action of the play is located simultaneously in mutually exclusive spaces and times—in the Mediterranean and in the Caribbean and yet in neither, exactly; in classical times and in the contemporary moment and yet not entirely in either.

This hybridity of geography and temporality, uneasily merging apparently irreconcilable differences, echoes both the play's plot and the generic hybridity I discussed at the beginning of this introduction. I suggested that *The Tempest* is the most characteristic play of the genre of romantic tragicomedy. By this I meant that, in its focus on reconciliation, its bringing together of comedy and tragedy, and its freedom with time and space, it embodies the typical energies of the genre that dominated the English stage both before and after the closure of the theaters during the English Civil War. I also suggested that the play is the least characteristic instance of this genre. By this I meant that its near-classical emphasis on the unities, its sustained resistance to the reconciliation to which it is oriented, and its dependence on magic rather than human agency for the unfolding of the plot make it a very different play from those that would follow—in particular the plays of John Fletcher, whose ethos is perhaps best expressed in a play called *The Custom of the Country* written a decade later than *The Tempest*, in which a pragmatic character bluntly informs his companion that "wonders are ceased; we must work by means."

Wonders cease at the end of *The Tempest*, but only after the impossible has been achieved. The play's magic demonstrates the value of the impossible for dramatic action, allowing Prospero to set up the action—to draw the usurper and his court to the island, to create the storm and the shipwreck, to move beyond the enclosing pattern of revenge—and yet permitting the audience to read the play as pure fiction. The impossible produces clarity, yet it also arguably confuses matters, too, mixing up for the audience the roles of human beings and of God in determining outcomes, with Prospero (who claims, blasphemously, to have raised the dead) poised uneasily between the mortal and the divine, powerful yet vulnerable. We have seen that though he can control the weather, he is threatened by human desire. Throughout the play, his magic seems only a partial or extreme way to counter individual agency and collective action. And, as we know, magic is illusion. There may be a harpy, a seeker for divine vengeance, in the action, but it is only a make-believe, constructed divinity, installed in the minds of the guilty, no more real than the "insubstantial pageant" of the masque. And we leave with the knowledge that in order to depart the island, Prospero has no choice but to renounce his magical powers, powers that we know to be impossible even as we benefit from their productivity. The play's shape as a dramatic text, the story it tells, and its role as an intervention in a political moment emerge from the same sense of the productivity of the impossible. It is the sense of openness this provokes, of slippage beyond the usual structures and restrictions of drama, that makes *The Tempest* so enigmatic, so beguiling, and so productive of further creativity.

Shakespeare and His England
by David Scott Kastan

hakespeare is a household name, one of those few that don't need a first name to be instantly recognized. His first name was, of course, William, and he (and it, in its Latin form, *Gulielmus*) first came to public notice on April 26, 1564, when his baptism was recorded in the parish church of Stratford-upon-Avon, a small market town about ninety miles northwest of London. It isn't known exactly when he was born, although traditionally his birthday is taken to be April 23rd. It is a convenient date (perhaps too convenient) because that was the date of his death in 1616, as well as the date of St. George's Day, the annual feast day of England's patron saint. It is possible Shakespeare was born on the 23rd; no doubt he was born within a day or two of that date. In a time of high rates of infant mortality, parents would not wait long after a baby's birth for the baptism. Twenty percent of all children would die before their first birthday.

Life in 1564, not just for infants, was conspicuously vulnerable. If one lived to age fifteen, one was likely to live into one's fifties, but probably no more than 60 percent of those born lived past their mid-teens. Whole towns could be ravaged by epidemic disease. In 1563, the year before Shakespeare was born, an outbreak of plague claimed over one third of the population of London. Fire, too, was a constant threat; the thatched roofs of many houses were highly flammable, as well as offering handy nesting places for insects and rats. Serious crop failures in several years of the decade of the 1560s created food short-ages, severe enough in many cases to lead to the starvation of the elderly and the infirm, and lowering the resistances of many others so that between 1536 and 1560 influenza claimed over 200,000 lives.

Shakespeare's own family in many ways reflected these unsettling realities. He was one of eight children, two of whom did not survive their first year, one of whom died at age eight; one lived to twenty-seven, while the four surviving siblings died at ages ranging from Edmund's thirty-nine to William's own fifty-two years. William married at an unusually early age. He was only eighteen, though his wife was twenty-six, almost exactly the norm of the day for women, though men normally married also in their mid- to late twenties. Shakespeare's wife Anne was already pregnant at the time that the marriage was formally confirmed, and a daughter, Susanna, was born six months later, in May 1583. Two years later, she gave birth to twins, Hamnet and Judith. Hamnet would die in his eleventh year.

If life was always at risk from what Shakespeare would later call "the thousand natural shocks / That flesh is heir to" (*Hamlet*, 3.1.61–62), the incessant threats to peace were no less unnerving, if usually less immediately life threatening. There were almost daily rumors of foreign invasion and civil war as the Protestant Queen Eliz-abeth assumed the crown in 1558 upon the death of her Catholic half sister, Mary. Mary's reign had been marked by the public burnings of Protestant "heretics," by the seeming subordination of England to Spain, and by a commitment to a ruinous war with France, that, among its other effects, fueled inflation and encouraged a debasing of the currency. If, for many, Elizabeth represented the hopes for a peaceful and prosperous Protestant future, it seemed unlikely in the early days of her rule that the young monarch could hold her England together against the twin menace of the powerful Catholic monarchies of Europe and the significant part of her own population who were reluctant to give up their old faith. No wonder the Queen's principal secretary saw England in the early years of Elizabeth's rule as a land surrounded by "perils many, great and imminent."

In Stratford-upon-Avon, it might often have been easy to forget what threatened from without. The simple rural life, shared by about 90 percent of the English populace, had its reassuring natural rhythms and delights. Life was structured by the daily rising and setting of the sun, and by the change of seasons. Crops were planted and harvested; livestock was bred, its young delivered; sheep were sheared, some livestock slaughtered. Market days and fairs saw the produce and crafts of the town arrayed as people came to sell and shop—and be entertained by musicians, dancers, and troupes of actors. But even in Stratford, the lurking tensions and dangers could be daily sensed. A few months before Shakespeare was born, there had been a shocking "defacing" of images in the church, as workmen, not content merely to whitewash over the religious paintings decorating the interior as they were ordered, gouged large holes in those felt to be too "Catholic"; a few months after Shakespeare's birth, the register of the same church records another deadly outbreak of plague. The sleepy market town on the northern bank of the gently flowing river Avon was not immune from the menace of the world that surrounded it.

This was the world into which Shakespeare was born. England at his birth was still poor and backward, a fringe nation on the periphery of Europe. English itself was a minor language, hardly spoken outside of the country's borders. Religious tension was inescapable, as the old Catholic faith was trying determinedly to hold on, even as Protestantism was once again anxiously trying to establish itself as the national religion. The country knew itself vulnerable to serious threats both from without and from within. In 1562, the young Queen, upon whom so many people's hopes rested, almost fell victim to smallpox, and in 1569 a revolt of the Northern earls tried to remove her from power and restore Catholicism as the national religion. The following year, Pope Pius V pronounced the excommunication of "Elizabeth, the pretended queen of England" and forbade Catholic subjects obedience to the monarch on pain of their own excommunication. "Now we are in an evil way and going to the devil," wrote one clergyman, "and have all nations in our necks."

It was a world of dearth, danger, and domestic unrest. Yet it would soon dramatically change, and Shakespeare's literary contribution would, for future generations, come to be seen as a significant measure of England's remarkable transformation. In the course of Shakespeare's life, England, hitherto an unsophisticated and underdeveloped backwater acting as a bit player in the momentous political dramas taking place on the European continent, became a confident, prosperous, global presence. But this new world was only accidentally, as it is often known today, "The Age of Shakespeare." To the degree that historical change rests in the hands of any individual, credit must be given to the Queen. This new world arguably was "The Age of Elizabeth," even if it was not the Elizabethan Golden Age, as it has often been portrayed.

The young Queen quickly imposed her personality upon the nation. She had talented councilors around her, all with strong ties to her of friendship or blood, but the direction of government was her own. She was strong willed and cautious, certain of her right to rule and convinced that stability was her greatest responsibility. The result may very well have been, as historians have often charged, that important issues facing England were never dealt with head-on and left to her successors to settle, but it meant also that she was able to keep her England unified and for the most part at peace.

Religion posed her greatest challenge, though it is important to keep in mind that in this period, as an official at Elizabeth's court said, "Religion and the commonwealth cannot be parted asunder." Faith then was not the largely voluntary commitment it is today, nor was there any idea of some separation of church and state. Religion was literally a matter of life and death, of salvation and damnation, and the Church was the Church of England. Obedience to it was not only a matter of conscience but also of law. It was the single issue on which the nation was most likely to be torn apart.

Elizabeth's great achievement was that she was successful in ensuring that the Church of England became formally a Protestant Church, but she did so without either driving most of her Catholic subjects to sedition or alienating the more radical Protestant community. The so-called "Elizabethan Settlement" forged a broad Christian community of what has been called prayer-book Protestantism, even as many of its practitioners retained, as a clergyman said, "still a smack and savor of popish principles." If there were forces on both sides who were uncomfortable with the Settlement—committed Protestants, who wanted to do away with all vestiges of the old faith, and convinced Catholics, who continued to swear their allegiance to Rome—the majority of the country, as she hoped, found ways to live comfortably both within the law and within their faith. In 1571, she wrote to the Duke of Anjou that the forms of worship she recommended would "not properly compel any man to alter his opinion in the great matters now in controversy in the Church." The official toleration of religious ambiguity, as well as the familiar experience of an official change of state religion accompanying the crowning of a new monarch, produced a world where the familiar labels of Protestant and Catholic failed to define the forms of faith that most English people practiced. But for Elizabeth, most matters of faith could be left to individuals, as long as the Church itself, and Elizabeth's position at its head, would remain unchallenged.

In international affairs, she was no less successful with her pragmatism and willingness to pursue limited goals. A complex mix of prudential concerns about religion, the economy, and national security drove her foreign policy. She did not have imperial ambitions; in the main, she wanted only to be sure there would be no invasion of England and to encourage English trade. In the event, both goals brought England into conflict with Spain, determining the increasingly anti-Catholic tendencies of English foreign policy and, almost accidentally, England's emergence as a world power. When Elizabeth came to the throne, England was in many ways a mere satellite nation to the Netherlands, which was part of the Hapsburg Empire that the Catholic Philip II (who had briefly and unhappily been married to her predecessor and half sister, Queen Mary) ruled from Spain; by the end of her reign England was Spain's most bitter rival.

The transformation of Spain from ally to enemy came in a series of small steps (or missteps), no one of which was intended to produce what in the end came to pass. A series of posturings and provocations on both sides led to the rupture. In 1568, things moved to their breaking point, as the English confiscated a large shipment of gold that the Spanish were sending to their troops in the Netherlands. The following year saw the revolt of the Catholic earls in Northern England, followed by the papal excommunication of the Queen in 1570, both of which were by many in England assumed to be at the initiative, or at very least with the tacit support, of Philip. In fact he was not involved, but England under Elizabeth would never again think of Spain as a loyal friend or reliable ally. Indeed, Spain quickly became its mortal enemy. Protestant Dutch rebels had been opposing the Spanish domination of the Netherlands since the early 1560s, but, other than periodic financial support, Elizabeth had done little to encourage them. But in 1585, she sent troops under the command of the Earl of Leicester to support the Dutch rebels against the Spanish. Philip decided then to launch a full-scale attack on England, with the aim of deposing Elizabeth and restoring the Catholic faith. An English assault on Cadiz in 1587 destroyed a number of Spanish ships, postponing Philip's plans, but in the summer of 1588 the mightiest navy in the world, Philip's grand armada, with 132 ships and 30,493 sailors and troops, sailed for England.

By all rights, it should have been a successful invasion, but a combination of questionable Spanish tactics and a fortunate shift of wind resulted in one of England's greatest victories. The English had twice failed to intercept the armada off the coast of Portugal, and the Spanish fleet made its way to England, almost catching the English ships resupplying in Plymouth. The English navy was on its heels, when conveniently the Spanish admiral decided to anchor in the English Channel off the French port of Calais to wait for additional troops coming from the Netherlands. The English attacked with fireships, sinking four Spanish galleons, and strong winds from the south prevented an effective counterattack from the Spanish. The Spanish fleet was pushed into the North Sea, where it regrouped and decided its safest course was to attempt the difficult voyage home around Scotland and Ireland, losing almost half its ships on the way. For many in England the improbable victory was a miracle, evidence of God's favor for Elizabeth and the Protestant nation. Though war with Spain would not end for another fifteen years, the victory over the armada turned England almost overnight into a major world power, buoyed by confidence that they were chosen by God and, more tangibly, by a navy that could compete for control of the seas.

From a backward and insignificant Hapsburg satellite, Elizabeth's England had become, almost by accident, the leader of Protestant Europe. But if the victory over the armada signaled England's new place in the world, it hardly marked the end of England's travails. The economy, which initially was fueled by the military buildup, in the early 1590s fell victim to inflation, heavy taxation to support the war with Spain, the inevitable wartime disruptions of trade, as well as crop failures and a general economic downturn in Europe. Ireland, over which England had been attempting to impose its rule since 1168, continued to be a source of trouble and great expense (in some years costing the crown nearly one fifth of its total revenues). Even when the most organized of the rebellions, begun in 1594 and led by Hugh O'Neill, Earl of Tyrone, formally ended in 1603, peace and stability had not been achieved.

But perhaps the greatest instability came from the uncertainty over the succession, an uncertainty that marked Elizabeth's reign from its beginning. Her near death from smallpox in 1562 reminded the nation that an unmarried queen could not insure the succession, and Elizabeth was under constant pressure to marry and produce an heir. She was always aware of and deeply resented the pressure, announcing as early as 1559: "this shall be for me sufficient that a marble stone shall declare that a queen, having reigned such a time, lived and died a virgin." If, however, it was for her "sufficient," it was not so for her advisors and for much of the nation, who hoped she would wed. Arguably Elizabeth was the wiser, knowing that her unmarried hand was a political advantage, allowing her to diffuse threats or create alliances with the seeming possibility of a match. But as with so much in her reign, the strategy bought temporary stability at the price of longer-term solutions.

By the mid 1590s, it was clear that she would die unmarried and without an heir, and various candidates were positioning themselves to succeed her. Enough anxiety was produced that all published debate about the succession was forbidden by law. There was no direct descendant of the English crown to claim rule, and all the claimants had to reach well back into their family history to find some legitimacy. The best genealogical claim belonged to King James VI of Scotland. His mother, Mary, Queen of Scots, was the granddaughter of James IV of Scotland and Margaret Tudor, sister to Elizabeth's father, Henry VIII. Though James had right on his side, he was, it must be remembered, a foreigner. Scotland shared the island with England but was a separate nation. Great Britain, the union of England and Scotland, would not exist formally until 1707, but with Elizabeth's death early in the morning of March 24, 1603, surprisingly uneventfully the thirty-seven-year-old James succeeded to the English throne. Two nations, one king: King James VI of Scotland, King James I of England.

Most of his English subjects initially greeted the announcement of their new monarch with delight, relieved that the crown had successfully been transferred without any major disruption and reassured that the new King was married with two living sons. However, quickly many became disenchanted with a foreign King who spoke English with a heavy accent, and dismayed even further by the influx of Scots in positions of power. Nonetheless, the new King's greatest political liability may well have been less a matter of nationality than of temperament: he had none of Elizabeth's skill and ease in publicly wooing her subjects. The Venetian ambassador wrote back to the doge that the new King was unwilling to "caress the people, nor make them that good cheer the late Queen did, whereby she won their loves."

He was aloof and largely uninterested in the daily activities of governing, but he was interested in political theory and strongly committed to the cause of peace. Although a steadfast Protestant, he lacked the reflexive anti-Catholicism of many of his subjects. In England, he achieved a broadly consensual community of Protestants. The so-called King James Bible, the famous translation published first in 1611, was the result of a widespread desire to have an English Bible that spoke to all the nation, transcending the religious divisions that had placed three different translations in the hands of his subjects. Internationally, he styled himself *Rex Pacificus* (the peace-loving king). In 1604, the Treaty of London brought Elizabeth's war with Spain formally to an end, and over the next decade he worked to bring about political marriages that might cement stable alliances. In 1613, he married his daughter to the leader of the German Protestants, while the following year he began discussions with Catholic Spain to marry his son to the Infanta Maria. After some ten years of negotiations, James's hopes for what was known as the Spanish match were finally abandoned, much to the delight of the nation, whose long-felt fear and hatred for Spain outweighed the subtle political logic behind the plan.

But if James sought stability and peace, and for the most part succeeded in his aims (at least until 1618, when the bitter religio-political conflicts on the European continent swirled well out of the

King's control), he never really achieved concord and cohesion. He ruled over two kingdoms that did not know, like, or even want to understand one another, and his rule did little to bring them closer together. His England remained separate from his Scotland, even as he ruled over both. And even his England remained self divided, as in truth it always was under Elizabeth, ever more a nation of prosperity and influence but still one forged out of deep-rooted divisions of means, faiths, and allegiances that made the very nature of English identity a matter of confusion and concern. Arguably this is the very condition of great drama—sufficient peace and prosperity to support a theater industry and sufficient provocation in the troubling uncertainties about what the nation was and what fundamentally mattered to its people to inspire plays that would offer tentative solutions or at the very least make the troubling questions articulate and moving.

Nine years before James would die in 1625, Shakespeare died, having returned from London to the small market town in which he was born. If London, now a thriving modern metropolis of well over 200,000 people, had, like the nation itself, been transformed in the course of his life, the Warwickshire market town still was much the same. The house in which Shakespeare was born still stood, as did the church in which he was baptized and the school in which he learned to read and write. The river Avon still ran slowly along the town's southern limits. What had changed was that Shakespeare was now its most famous citizen, and, although it would take more than another 100 years to fully achieve this, he would in time become England's, for having turned the great ethical, social, and political issues of his own age into plays that would live forever.

William Shakespeare:
A Chronology

1558	**November 17: Queen Elizabeth crowned**
1564	April 26: Shakespeare baptized, third child born to John Shakespeare and Mary Arden
1564	**May 27: Death of Jean Calvin in Geneva**
1565	John Shakespeare elected alderman in Stratford-upon-Avon
1568	**Publication of the Bishops' Bible**
1568	September 4: John Shakespeare elected Bailiff of Stratford-upon-Avon
1569	**Northern Rebellion**
1570	**Queen Elizabeth excommunicated by the pope**
1572	**August 24: St. Bartholomew's Day Massacre in Paris**
1577–1580	**Sir Francis Drake sails around the world**
1582	November 27: Shakespeare and Anne Hathaway married (Shakespeare is 18)
1583	Queen's Men formed
1583	May 26: Shakespeare's daughter, Susanna, baptized
1584	**Failure of the Virginia Colony**
1585	February 2: Twins, Hamnet and Judith, baptized (Shakespeare is 20)

1586   **Babington Plot to dethrone Elizabeth and replace her with Mary, Queen of Scots**

1587   **February 8: Execution of Mary, Queen of Scots**

1587   **Rose Theatre built**

1588   **August: Defeat of the Spanish armada** (Shakespeare is 24)

1588   **September 4: Death of Robert Dudley, Earl of Leicester**

1590   **First three books of Spenser's *Faerie Queene* published; Marlowe's *Tamburlaine* published**

1592   March 3: *Henry VI, Part One* performed at the Rose Theatre (Shakespeare is 27)

1593   **February–November: Theaters closed because of plague**

1593   Publication of *Venus and Adonis*

1594   Publication of *Titus Andronicus*, first play by Shakespeare to appear in print (though anonymously)

1594   Lord Chamberlain's Men formed

1595   March 15: Payment made to Shakespeare, Will Kemp, and Richard Burbage for performances at court in December, 1594

1595   **Swan Theatre built**

1596   **Books 4–6 of *The Faerie Queene* published**

1596   August 11: Burial of Shakespeare's son, Hamnet (Shakespeare is 32)

1596–1599   Shakespeare living in St. Helen's, Bishopsgate, London

1596   October 20: Grant of Arms to John Shakespeare

1597   May 4: Shakespeare purchases New Place, one of the two largest houses in Stratford (Shakespeare is 33)

1598   Publication of *Love's Labor's Lost*, first extant play with Shakespeare's name on the title page

1598   Publication of Francis Meres's *Palladis Tamia*, citing Shakespeare as "the best for Comedy and Tragedy" among English writers

1599   **Opening of the Globe Theatre**

1601   **February 7: Lord Chamberlain's Men paid 40 shillings to play *Richard II* by supporters of the Earl of Essex, the day before his abortive rebellion**

1601   **February 17: Execution of Robert Devereaux, Earl of Essex**

1601   September 8: Burial of John Shakespeare

1602   May 1: Shakespeare buys 107 acres of farmland in Stratford

1603   **March 24: Queen Elizabeth dies; James VI of Scotland succeeds as James I of England** (Shakespeare is 39)

1603   May 19: Lord Chamberlain's Men reformed as the King's Men

1604   Shakespeare living with the Mountjoys, a French Huguenot family, in Cripplegate, London

1604   **First edition of Marlowe's *Dr. Faustus* published (written c. 1589)**

1604   March 15: Shakespeare named among "players" given scarlet cloth to wear at royal procession of King James

1604   Publication of authorized version of *Hamlet* (Shakespeare is 40)

1605   **Gunpowder Plot**

1605   June 5: Marriage of Susanna Shakespeare to John Hall

1608   Publication of *King Lear* (Shakespeare is 44)

1608–1609   Acquisition of indoor Blackfriars Theatre by King's Men

1609   *Sonnets* published

1611   **King James Bible published** (Shakespeare is 47)

1612   **November 6: Death of Henry, eldest son of King James**

1613   **February 14: Marriage of King James's daughter Elizabeth
to Frederick, the Elector Palatine**

1613   March 10: Shakespeare, with some associates, buys gatehouse
in Blackfriars, London

1613   **June 29: Fire burns the Globe Theatre**

1614   **Rebuilt Globe reopens**

1616   February 10: Marriage of Judith Shakespeare to Thomas Quiney

1616   March 25: Shakespeare's will signed

1616   April 23: Shakespeare dies (age 52)

1616   **April 23: Cervantes dies in Madrid**

1616   April 25: Shakespeare buried in Holy Trinity Church in
Stratford-upon-Avon

1623   August 6: Death of Anne Shakespeare

1623   **October: King James returns from Madrid, having failed
to marry his son Charles to Maria Anna, Infanta of Spain**

1623   First Folio published with 36 plays (18 never previously published)

Words, Words, Words: Understanding Shakespeare's Language
by David Scott Kastan

t is silly to pretend that it is easy to read Shakespeare. Reading Shakespeare isn't like picking up a copy of *USA Today* or *The New Yorker*, or even F. Scott Fitzgerald's *Great Gatsby* or Toni Morrison's *Beloved*. It is hard work, because the language is often unfamiliar to us and because it is more concentrated than we are used to. In the theater it is usually a bit easier. Actors can clarify meanings with gestures and actions, allowing us to get the general sense of what is going on, if not every nuance of the language that is spoken. "Action is eloquence," as Volumnia puts it in *Coriolanus*, "and the eyes of th' ignorant / More learnèd than the ears" (3.276–277). Yet the real greatness of Shakespeare rests not on "the general sense" of his plays but on the specificity and suggestiveness of the words in which they are written. It is through language that the plays' full dramatic power is realized, and it is that rich and robust language, often pushed by Shakespeare to the very limits of intelligibility, that we must learn to understand. But we can come to understand it (and enjoy it), and this essay is designed to help.

Even experienced readers and playgoers need help. They often find that his words are difficult to comprehend. Shakespeare sometimes uses words no longer current in English or with meanings that have changed. He regularly multiplies words where seemingly one might do as well or even better. He characteristically writes sentences that are syntactically complicated and imaginatively dense. And it isn't just we, removed by some 400 years from his world, who find him difficult to read; in his own time, his friends and fellow actors knew Shakespeare was hard. As two of them, John Hemings and Henry Condell, put it in their prefatory remarks to Shakespeare's First Folio in 1623, "read him, therefore, and again and again; and if then you do not like him, surely you are in some manifest danger not to understand him."

From the very beginning, then, it was obvious that the plays both deserve and demand not only careful reading but continued re-reading—and that not to read Shakespeare with all the attention a reader can bring to bear on the language is almost to guarantee that a reader will not "understand him" and remain among those who "do not like him." But Shakespeare's colleagues were nonetheless confident that the plays exerted an attraction strong enough to ensure and reward the concentration of their readers, confident, as they say, that in them "you will find enough, both to draw and hold you." The plays do exert a kind of magnetic pull, and have successfully drawn in and held readers for over 400 years.

Once we are drawn in, we confront a world of words that does not always immediately yield its delights; but it will—once we learn to see what is demanded of us. Words in Shakespeare do a lot, arguably more than anyone else has ever asked them to do. In part, it is because he needed his words to do many things at once. His stage had no sets and few props, so his words are all we have to enable us to imagine what his characters see. And they also allow us to see what the characters don't see, especially about themselves. The words are vivid and immediate, as well as complexly layered and psychologically suggestive. The difficulties they pose are not the "thee's" and "thou's" or "prithee's" and "doth's" that obviously mark the chronological distance between Shakespeare and us. When

Gertrude says to Hamlet, "thou hast thy father much offended" (3.4.8), we have no difficulty understanding her chiding, though we might miss that her use of the "thou" form of the pronoun expresses an intimacy that Hamlet pointedly refuses with his reply: "Mother, *you* have my father much offended" (3.4.9; italics mine).

Most deceptive are words that look the same as words we know but now mean something different. Words often change meanings over time. When Horatio and the soldiers try to stop Hamlet as he chases after the Ghost, Hamlet pushes past them and says, "I'll make a ghost of him that lets me" (1.4.85). It seems an odd thing to say. Why should he threaten someone who "lets" him do what he wants to do? But here "let" means "hinder," not, as it does today, "allow" (although the older meaning of the word still survives, for example, in tennis, where a "let serve" is one that is hindered by the net on its way across). There are many words that can, like this, mislead us: "his" sometimes means "its," "an" often means "if," "envy" means something more like "malice," "cousin" means more generally "kinsman," and there are others, though all are easily defined. The difficulty is that we may not stop to look thinking we already know what the word means, but in this edition a ° following the word alerts a reader that there is a gloss in the left margin, and quickly readers get used to these older meanings.

Then, of course, there is the intimidation factor—strange, polysyllabic, or Latinate words that not only are foreign to us but also must have sounded strange even to Shakespeare's audiences. When Macbeth wonders whether all the water in all the oceans of the world will be able to clean his bloody hands after the murder of Duncan, he concludes: "No; this my hand will rather / The multitudinous seas incarnadine, / Making the green one red" (2.2.64–66). Duncan's blood staining Macbeth's murderous hand is so offensive that, not merely does it resist being washed off in water, but it will "the multitudinous seas incarnadine": that is, turn the sea-green oceans blood-red. Notes will easily clarify the meaning of the two odd words, but it is worth observing that they would have been as odd to Shakespeare's readers as they are to us. The *Oxford English Dictionary (OED)* shows no use of "multitudinous" before this, and it records no use of "incarnadine" before 1591 (*Macbeth* was written about 1606). Both are new words, coined from the Latin, part of a process in Shakespeare's time where English adopted many Latinate words as a mark of its own emergence as an important vernacular language. Here they are used to express the magnitude of Macbeth's offense, a crime not only against the civil law but also against the cosmic order, and then the simple monosyllables of turning "the green one red" provide an immediate (and needed) paraphrase and register his own, sickening awareness of the true hideousness of his deed.

As with "multitudinous" in *Macbeth*, Shakespeare is the source of a great many words in English. Sometimes he coined them himself, or, if he didn't invent them, he was the first person whose writing of them has survived. Some of these words have become part of our language, so common that it is hard to imagine they were not always part of it: for example, "assassination" (*Macbeth*, 1.7.2), "bedroom" (*A Midsummer Night's Dream*, 2.2.57), "countless" (*Titus Andronicus*, 5.3.59), "fashionable" (*Troilus and Cressida*, 3.3.165), "frugal" (*The Merry Wives of Windsor*, 2.1.28), "laughable" (*The Merchant of Venice*, 1.1.56), "lonely" (*Coriolanus*, 4.1.30), and "useful" (*King John*, 5.2.81). But other words that he originated were not as, to use yet another Shakespearean coinage, "successful" (*Titus Andronicus*, 1.1.66). Words like "crimeless" (*Henry VI, Part Two*, 2.4.63, meaning "innocent"), "facinorous" (*All's Well That Ends Well*, 2.3.30, meaning "extremely wicked"), and "recountment" (*As You Like It*, 4.3.141, meaning "narrative" or "account") have, without much resistance, slipped into oblivion. Clearly Shakespeare liked words, even unwieldy ones. His working vocabulary, about 18,000 words, is staggering, larger than almost any other English writer, and he seems to be the first person to use in print about

1,000 of these. Whether he coined the new words himself or was intrigued by the new words he heard in the streets of London doesn't really matter; the point is that he was remarkably alert to and engaged with a dynamic language that was expanding in response to England's own expanding contact with the world around it.

But it is neither new words nor old ones that are the source of the greatest difficulty of Shakespeare's language. The real difficulty (and the real delight) comes in trying to see how he uses the words, how he endows them with more than their denotative meanings. Why, for example, does Macbeth say that he hopes that the "sure and firm-set earth" (2.1.56) will not hear his steps as he goes forward to murder Duncan? Here "sure" and "firm-set" mean virtually the same thing: stable, secure, fixed. Why use two words? If this were a student paper, no doubt the teacher would circle one of them and write "redundant." But the redundancy is exactly what Shakespeare wants. One word would do if the purpose were to describe the solidity of the earth, but here the redundancy points to something different. It reveals something about Macbeth's mind, betraying through the doubling how deep is his awareness of the world of stable values that the terrible act he is about to commit must unsettle.

Shakespeare's words usually work this way: in part describing what the characters see and as often betraying what they feel. The example from *Macbeth* is a simple example of how this works. Shakespeare's words are carefully patterned. How one says something is every bit as important as what is said, and the conspicuous patterns that are created alert us to the fact that something more than the words' lexical sense has been put into play. Words can be coupled, as in the example above, or knit into even denser metaphorical constellations to reveal something about the speaker (which often the speaker does not know), as in Prince Hal's promise to his father that he will outdo the rebels' hero, Henry Percy (Hotspur):

Percy is but my factor, good my lord,
To engross up glorious deeds on my behalf,
And I will call him to so strict account
That he shall render every glory up,
Yea, even the slightest worship of his time,
Or I will tear the reckoning from his heart.

(Henry IV, Part One, 3.2.147–152)

The Prince expresses his confidence that he will defeat Hotspur, but revealingly in a reiterated language of commercial exchange ("factor," "engross," "account," "render," "reckoning") that tells us something important both about the Prince and the ways in which he understands his world. In a play filled with references to coins and counterfeiting, the speech demonstrates not only that Hal has committed himself to the business at hand, repudiating his earlier, irresponsible tavern self, but also that he knows it is a business rather than a glorious world of chivalric achievement; he inhabits a world in which value (political as well as economic) is not intrinsic but determined by what people are willing to invest, and he proves himself a master of producing desire for what he has to offer.

Or sometimes it is not the network of imagery but the very syntax that speaks, as when Claudius announces his marriage to Hamlet's mother:

Therefore our sometime sister, now our Queen,
Th' imperial jointress to this warlike state,
Have we—as 'twere with a defeated joy,
With an auspicious and a dropping eye,
With mirth in funeral and with dole in marriage,
In equal scale weighing delight and dole—
Taken to wife.

(Hamlet, 1.2.8–14)

All he really wants to say here is that he has married Gertrude, his former sister-in-law: "Therefore our sometime sister . . . Have we . . . Taken to wife." But the straightforward sentence gets interrupted and complicated, revealing his own discomfort with the announcement. His elaborations and intensifications of Gertrude's role ("sometime sister," "Queen," "imperial jointress"), the self-conscious rhetorical balancing of the middle three lines (indeed "in equal scale weighing delight and dole"), all declare by the all-too obvious artifice how desperate he is to hide the awkward facts behind a veneer of normalcy and propriety. The very unnaturalness of the sentence is what alerts us that we are meant to understand more than the simple relation of fact.

Why doesn't Shakespeare just say what he means? Well, he does—exactly what he means. In the example from *Hamlet* just above, Shakespeare shows us something about Claudius that Claudius doesn't know himself. Always Shakespeare's words will offer us an immediate sense of what is happening, allowing us to follow the action, but they also offer us a counterplot, pointing us to what might be behind the action, confirming or contradicting what the characters say. It is a language that shimmers with promise and possibility, opening the characters' hearts and minds to our view—and all we have to do is learn to pay attention to what is there before us.

Shakespeare's Verse

Another distinctive feature of Shakespeare's dramatic language is that much of it is in verse. Almost all of the plays mix poetry and prose, but the poetry dominates. *The Merry Wives of Windsor* has the lowest percentage (only about 13 percent verse), while *Richard II* and *King John* are written entirely in verse (the only examples, although *Henry VI, Part One* and *Part Three* have only a very few prose lines). In most of the plays, about 70 percent of the lines are written in verse.

Shakespeare's characteristic verse line is a non-rhyming iambic pentameter ("blank verse"), ten syllables with every second one stressed. In *A Midsummer Night's Dream*, Titania comes to her senses after a magic potion has led her to fall in love with an ass-headed Bottom: "Methought I was enamored of an ass" (4.1.76). Similarly, in *Romeo and Juliet*, Romeo gazes up at Juliet's window: "But soft, what light through yonder window breaks" (2.2.2). In both these examples, the line has ten syllables organized into five regular beats (each beat consisting of the stress on the second syllable of a pair, as in "But soft," the da-dum rhythm forming an "iamb"). Still, we don't hear these lines as jingles; they seem natural enough, in large part because this dominant pattern is varied in the surrounding lines.

The play of stresses indeed becomes another key to meaning, as Shakespeare alerts us to what is important. In *Measure for Measure*, Lucio urges Isabella to plead for her brother's life: "Oh, to him, to him, wench! He will relent" (2.2.129). The iambic norm (unstressed-stressed) tells us (and an actor) that the emphasis at the beginning of the line is on "to" not "him"—it is the action not the object that is being emphasized—and at the end of the line the stress falls on "will." Alternatively, the line can play against the established norm. In *Hamlet*, Claudius corrects Polonius's idea of what is bothering the Prince: "Love? His affections do not that way tend" (3.1.161). The iambic norm forces the emphasis onto "that" ("do not *that* way tend"), while the syntax forces an unexpected stress on the opening word, "Love." In the famous line, "The course of true love never did run smooth" (*A Midsummer Night's Dream*, 1.1.134), the iambic expectation is varied in both the middle and at the end of the line. Both "love" and the first syllable of "never" are stressed, as are both syllables at the end: "run smooth," creating a metrical foot in which both syllables are stressed (called a "spondee"). The point to notice is that the "da-dum, da-dum, da-dum, da-dum, da-dum" line is not inevitable; it merely sets an expectation against which many variations can be heard.

In fact, even the ten-syllable norm can be varied. Shakespeare sometimes writes lines with fewer or more syllables. Often there is an extra, unstressed syllable at the end of a line (a so-called "feminine ending"); sometimes there are verse lines with only nine. In *Henry IV, Part One*, King Henry replies incredulously to the rebel Worcester's claim that he hadn't "sought" the confrontation with the King: "You have not sought it? How comes it then?" (5.1.27). There are only nine syllables here (some earlier editors, seeking to "correct" the verse, added the word "sir" after the first question to regularize the line). But the pause where one expects a stressed syllable is dramatically effective, allowing the King's anger to be powerfully present in the silence.

As even these few examples show, Shakespeare's verse is unusually flexible, allowing a range of rhythmical effects. It should not be understood as a set of strict rules but as a flexible set of practices rooted in dramatic necessity. It is designed to highlight ideas and emotions, and it is based less upon rigid syllable counts than on an arrangement of stresses within an understood temporal norm, as one might expect from a poetry written to be heard in the theater rather than read on the page.

Here Follows Prose

Although the plays are dominated by verse, prose plays a significant role. Shakespeare's prose has its own rhythms, but it lacks the formal patterning of verse, and so is printed without line breaks and without the capitals that mark the beginning of a verse line. Like many of his fellow dramatists, Shakespeare tended to use prose for comic scenes, the shift from verse serving, especially in his early plays, as a social marker. Upper-class characters speak in verse; lower-class characters speak in prose. Thus, in *A Midsummer Night's Dream*, the Athenians of the court, as well as the fairies, all speak in verse, but the "rude mechanicals," Bottom and his artisan friends, all speak in prose, except for the comic verse they speak in their performance of "Pyramis and Thisbe."

As Shakespeare grew in experience, he became more flexible about the shifts from verse to prose, letting it, among other things, mark genre rather than class and measure various kinds of intensity. Prose becomes in the main the medium of comedy. The great comedies, like *Much Ado About Nothing*, *Twelfth Night*, and *As You Like It*, are all more than 50 percent prose. But even in comedy, shifts between verse and prose may be used to measure subtle emotional changes. In Act One, scene three of *The Merchant of Venice*, Shylock and Bassanio begin the scene speaking of matters of business in prose, but when Antonio enters and the deep conflict between the Christian and the Jew becomes evident, the scene shifts to verse. But prose may itself serve in moments of emotional intensity. Shylock's famous speech in Act Three, scene one, "Hath not a Jew eyes . . ." is all in prose, as is Hamlet's expression of disgust at the world ("I have of late— but wherefore I know not—lost all my mirth . . .") at 3.1.261–276. Shakespeare comes to use prose to vary the tone of a scene, as the shift from verse subtly alerts an audience or a reader to some new emotional register.

Prose becomes, as Shakespeare's art matures, not inevitably the mark of the lower classes but the mark of a salutary daily-ness. It is appropriately the medium in which letters are written, and it is the medium of a common sense that will at least challenge the potential self-deceptions of grandiloquent speech. When Rosalind mocks the excesses and artifice of Orlando's wooing in Act Four, scene one of *As You Like It*, it is in prose that she seeks something genuine in the expression of love:

The poor world is almost six thousand years old, and in all this time there was not any man died in his own person, *videlicit* [i.e., namely], in a love cause. . . . Men have died from time to time, and worms have eaten them, but not for love.

Here the prose becomes the sound of common sense, an effective foil to the affectation of pinning poems to trees and thinking that it is real love.

It is not that prose is artless; Shakespeare's prose is no less self-conscious than his verse. The artfulness of his prose is different, of course. The seeming ordinariness of his prose is no less an effect of his artistry than is the more obvious patterning of his verse. Prose is no less serious, compressed, or indeed figurative. As with his verse, Shakespeare's prose performs numerous tasks and displays various, subtle formal qualities; and recognizing the possibilities of what it can achieve is still another way of seeing what Shakespeare puts right before us to show us what he has hidden.

Further Reading

N. F. Blake, *Shakespeare's Language*: An Introduction (New York: St. Martin's Press, 1983).

Jonathan Hope, *Shakespeare's Grammar* (London: Thomson, 2003).

Sister Miriam Joseph, *Shakespeare's Use of the Arts of Language* (New York: Columbia University Press, 1947).

M. M. Mahood, *Shakespeare's Wordplay* (London: Methuen, 1957).

Russ McDonald, *Shakespeare and the Arts of Language* (Oxford: Oxford University Press, 2001).

Brian Vickers, *The Artistry of Shakespeare's Prose* (London: Methuen, 1968).

George T. Wright, *Shakespeare's Metrical Art* (Univ. of California Press, 1991).

Key to the Play Text

Symbols

o	Indicates an explanation or definition in the left-hand margin.
1	Indicates a gloss on the page facing the play text.
[ ]	Indicates something added or changed by the editors (i.e., not in the early printed text that this edition of the play is based on).

Terms

F, *Folio*, or *First Folio*	The first collected edition of Shakespeare's plays, published in 1623. *The Tempest* was first published in the 1623 Folio.
Q, *Quarto*	The usual format in which the individual plays were first published.

The Tempest

William Shakespeare

List of Roles

Alonso	*King of Naples*
Sebastian	*his brother*
Prospero	*the right Duke of Milan*
Antonio	*his brother, the usurping Duke of Milan*
Ferdinand	*son of the King of Naples*
Gonzalo	*an honest old councilor*
Adrian and Francisco	*lords*
Caliban	*a savage and deformed slave*
Trinculo	*a jester*
Stephano	*a drunken butler*
Master	*of a ship*
Boatswain	*of the ship*
Mariners	*of the ship*
Miranda	*daughter of Prospero*
Ariel	*an airy spirit*
Iris	*a spirit*
Ceres	*a spirit*
Juno	*a spirit*
Nymphs	*spirits*
Reapers	*spirits*

1   *Boatswain*

    **(Pronounced BO-sun); subordinate
    officer on a ship responsible for the
    hull and equipment**

2   *What cheer?*

    **What's your mood? (How are
    things going?)**

3   *Good*

    **I.e., good man (as in 1.1.14, or
    possibly a perfunctory answer to
    line 2)**

4   *bestir*

    Stir yourself; i.e., get going

5   *cheerly, my hearts*

    **Keep up your effort with good
    cheer, my hearty men**

6   *Blow*

    **The boatswain defiantly addresses
    the wind itself.**

7   *if room enough*

    **I.e., as long as you (i.e., the wind)
    don't push us too close to the rocks**

8   *Play the men!*

    **Either "act like real men" or "get to
    work"**

9   *You mar our labor.*

    You're disturbing our work.

Act 1, Scene 1

A tempestuous noise of thunder and lightning heard.

Enter a ship **Master** *and a* **Boatswain**.

Master

Boatswain![1]

Boatswain

captain   Here, master.° What cheer?[2]

Master

right away   Good,[3] speak to th' mariners. Fall to 't yarely,° or we
run ourselves aground. Bestir, bestir.[4]   *He exits.*

Enter **Mariners**.

Boatswain

Quick!   Heigh, my hearts! Cheerly, cheerly, my hearts![5] Yare!°   5
Yare! Take in the topsail. Tend to th' master's whistle.
—Blow[6] till thou burst thy wind, if room enough![7]

Enter **Alonso**, **Sebastian**, **Antonio**, **Ferdinand**,
Gonzalo, *and others.*

Alonso

Good boatswain, have care. Where's the master?
[*To the* **Mariners**] Play the men![8]

Boatswain

urge you   I pray° now keep below!   10

Antonio

Where is the master, boatswain?

Boatswain

Keep to   Do you not hear him? You mar our labor.[9] Keep° your
cabins! You do assist the storm.

1   *roarers*

A term denoting both natural and
social disruption. On one level the
roaring is simply the noise of thunder
or the sound the waves are making,
but the word also invokes the idea of
a "roaring boy" (or, in Middleton and
Dekker's play of that name, a "roaring
girl"), that is, a riotous and
quarrelsome urban youth with no
respect for order or authority.

2   *work the peace of the present*

I.e., make the present moment a
peaceful one.

3   *make yourself ready in your cabin for the*
     mischance of the hour, if it so hap.

Prepare yourselves for the
calamities of the moment, if they
should occur.

4   *he hath no drowning mark upon him. His*
     complexion is perfect gallows.

I.e., he doesn't have the look of a
man about to drown; his face
seems perfectly suited for the
gallows. Gonzalo is alluding to the
proverb, "He that is born to be
hanged shall never be drowned."

5   *Stand fast, good fate, to his hanging.*
     Make the rope of his destiny our cable,
     for our own doth little advantage.

Good fate, stay committed to the
boatswain's destiny to hang (rather
than to drown). Let the hangman's
rope become our support, since
our own ropes do us little good.

6   *Bring her to try with main course*

I.e., direct the boat close to the
wind, using the mainsail.

Gonzalo

Nay, good, be patient.

Boatswain

When the sea is. Hence! What cares these roarers[1] for   15
the name of king? To cabin! Silence! Trouble us not.

Gonzalo

Good, yet remember whom thou hast aboard.

Boatswain

advisor   None that I more love than myself. You are a councilor.° If
you can command these elements to silence and work
handle   the peace of the present,[2] we will not hand° a rope   20
more. Use your authority. If you cannot, give thanks
you have lived so long and make yourself ready in your
cabin for the mischance of the hour, if it so hap.[3]
—Cheerly, good hearts!—Out of our way, I say.   *He exits.*

Gonzalo

I have great comfort from this fellow. Methinks he   25
hath no drowning mark upon him. His complexion is
perfect gallows.[4] Stand fast, good fate, to his hanging.
Make the rope of his destiny our cable, for our own
doth little advantage.[5] If he be not born to be hanged,
our case is miserable.   *He exits [with courtiers].*   30

Enter **Boatswain**.

Boatswain

Down with the topmast! Yare, lower, lower! Bring her
to try with main course.[6]   *(A cry within.)*
i.e., The passengers   A plague upon this howling! They° are louder than the
own work   weather or our office.°

Enter **Sebastian**, **Antonio**, *and* **Gonzalo**.

1   *Work you*

    Either "get to work to help me" or "I
    dare you to get your curse to work on
    me"

2   *I'll warrant him for drowning*

    I'll guarantee that he won't drown

3   *unstanched*

    The word may mean both
    "insatiable" or "not water-tight," so
    refers either to a woman whose
    sexual appetite cannot be controlled
    or to a menstruating woman.

4   *Lay her a-hold, a-hold! Set her two
    courses off to sea again!*

    Maneuver the ship into the wind.
    Let out the topsail and the mainsail
    and move out to sea again!

5   *would thou mightst lie drowning the
    washing of ten tides*

    I.e., I wish you were left to drown
    through the course of ten tides.
    Convicted pirates were hanged and
    then left on shore for the length of
    three tides.

up   Yet again? What do you here? Shall we give o'er° and   35

       drown? Have you a mind to sink?

Sebastian

curse   A pox° o' your throat, you bawling, blasphemous,

       incharitable dog!

Boatswain

       Work you¹ then.

Antonio

vile   Hang, cur! Hang, you whoreson,° insolent noise-   40

       maker! We are less afraid to be drowned than thou art.

Gonzalo

even if   I'll warrant him for drowning² though° the ship were

       no stronger than a nutshell and as leaky as an

       unstanched³ wench.

Boatswain

       Lay her a-hold, a-hold! Set her two courses off to sea   45

       again!⁴ Lay her off!

           Enter **Mariners**, *wet*.

Mariners

       All lost! To prayers, to prayers! All lost!   [*They exit.*]

Boatswain

i.e., in death   What? Must our mouths be cold?°

Gonzalo

       The King and Prince at prayers—let's assist them, for

       our case is as theirs.   50

Sebastian

       I'm out of patience.

Antonio

completely   We are merely° cheated of our lives by drunkards.

square-jawed   This wide-chopped° rascal—would thou mightst lie

       drowning the washing of ten tides!⁵

1. *He'll be hanged yet, though every drop of water swear against it and gape at widest to glut him.*

   He'll still die by hanging, even if the water swears otherwise and opens its mouth as wide as possible to swallow him.

2. *We split*

   The boat is splitting apart.

3. *take leave of*

   Say good-bye to

4. *wills above*

   I.e., the will of God

Gonzalo

He'll be hanged yet, though every drop of water swear 55
against it and gape at widest to glut him. [1]

A confused noise within.

Voices

[*within*] Mercy on us!—We split; [2] we split!—Farewell,
my wife and children!—Farewell, brother!—We split;
we split; we split!

Antonio

Let's all sink wi' th' King. 60

Sebastian

Let's take leave of [3] him. *He exits [with* **Antonio**].

Gonzalo

Now would I give a thousand furlongs of sea for an acre
heather/gorse of barren ground: long heath,° brown furze,° anything.
rather The wills above [4] be done, but I would fain° die a dry death.

He exits.

1 **Prospero**

"Fortunate" or "favorable" in Italian

2 **Miranda**

From the Latin for "to be wondered at"

3 *The sky, it seems, would pour down stinking*
pitch / But that the sea, mounting to th'
welkin's cheek, / Dashes the fire out.

I.e., the sky is so dark that it seems as
if it will rain foul-smelling tar (*pitch*),
except that the waves, which reach
up to the edge of the sky, have
extinguished the lightning (that
would turn the pitch to liquid).

4 *or ere*

Before

5 *fraughting souls*

I.e., the people who are the ship's
freight, or cargo

6 *but in care of thee*

That wasn't for your benefit

7 *naught knowing / Of whence I am, nor that*
I am more better / Than Prospero, master of
a full poor cell, / And thy no greater father

Knowing nothing of where I come
from, nor that I am greater than
simply Prospero, master of this
humble dwelling and a father of no
great account

Act 1, Scene 2

Enter **Prospero** [1] *and* **Miranda**. [2]

Miranda

i.e., magic   If by your art,° my dearest father, you have

calm   Put the wild waters in this roar, allay° them.

The sky, it seems, would pour down stinking pitch

sky's   But that the sea, mounting to th' welkin's° cheek,

Dashes the fire out. [3] Oh, I have suffered   5

handsome; well-made   With those that I saw suffer. A brave° vessel

(Who had, no doubt, some noble creature in her)

Dashed all to pieces. Oh, the cry did knock

Against my very heart! Poor souls, they perished.

Had I been any god of power, I would   10

Have sunk the sea within the earth or ere [4]

It should the good ship so have swallowed and

The fraughting souls [5] within her.

Prospero

                           Be collected.°

composed; calm

astonishment   No more amazement.° Tell your piteous heart

There's no harm done.

Miranda

                    Oh, woe the day!

Prospero

                            No harm.   15

I have done nothing but in care of thee, [6]

Of thee, my dear one, thee, my daughter, who

Art ignorant of what thou art, naught knowing

Of whence I am, nor that I am more better

Than Prospero, master of a full poor cell,   20

And thy no greater father. [7]

1 *More to know / Did never meddle with
my thoughts.*

It never occurred to me to find
out more.

2 *Lie there, my art.*

Prospero speaks to his cloak, with
its magical properties.

3 *with such provision in mine art*

By exercising great foresight while
deploying my magic

4 *So safely ordered that*

So carefully organized (this
shipwreck) that

5 *not so much perdition as an hair / Betid
to any creature in the vessel*

No creature on board lost even so
much as a hair. This phrase is
grammatically independent of
what precedes and follows the
dashes: Prospero interrupts and
reiterates himself.

6 *left me to a bootless inquisition*

Left my questions unanswered

7 *cell*

Miranda and Prospero's hut; in the
16th century, the word *cell* referred to
a humble dwelling (or, more
specifically, a single-roomed
monastic residence) and hadn't yet
become associated with
imprisonment.

Miranda

More to know
Did never meddle with my thoughts. [1]

Prospero

'Tis time
I should inform thee farther. Lend thy hand
And pluck my magic garment from me.

[**Miranda** *helps* **Prospero** *remove his mantle.*]

So;
Lie there, my art. [2]—Wipe thou thine eyes. Have comfort.   25
wreck   The direful spectacle of the wrack,° which touched
The very virtue of compassion in thee,
I have with such provision in mine art [3]
So safely ordered that [4] there is no soul—
loss   No, not so much perdition° as an hair   30
Happened   Betid° to any creature in the vessel [5]—
Which thou heard'st cry, which thou saw'st sink. Sit down,
For thou must now know farther.

Miranda

You have often
Begun to tell me what I am, but stopped
And left me to a bootless inquisition, [6]   35
Concluding, "Stay. Not yet."

Prospero

The hour's now come.
open   The very minute bids thee ope° thine ear.
Obey and be attentive. Canst thou remember
A time before we came unto this cell? [7]
I do not think thou canst, for then thou wast not   40
Fully   Out° three years old.

Miranda

Certainly, sir, I can.

1   *Of any thing the image tell me that /*
    Hath kept with thy remembrance.

    **Describe to me any image you can
    remember.**

2   *rather like a dream than an assurance /*
    That my remembrance warrants

    **More like a dream than an
    objective fact that my memory can
    guarantee**

3   *How thou cam'st here thou mayst*

    **Then you may also remember how
    you came here**

4   *Milan*

    **Emphasis on the first syllable. Italy,
    in Shakespeare's time, was not a
    single country but a series of city-
    states, of which Milan in the north
    and Naples in the south were two of
    the most prominent. In the 16th
    century, however, Milan was under
    the control first of France and then
    of Spain, and, by the time *The Tempest*
    was written, the Neopolitan dynasty
    of the Aragonese family had been
    displaced by Spanish governors. The
    dominant family in Milan in the
    Renaissance were the Sforzas, and
    their palace, the Castello Sforza, is
    one of the city's tourist sites now;
    perhaps Prospero is envisaged as a
    member of this family, whose name
    would have been known in England.**

5   *princess no worse issued*

    As nobly born as a princess

Prospero

By what? By any other house or person?
Of any thing the image tell me that
Hath kept with thy remembrance. [1]

Miranda

'Tis far off
And rather like a dream than an assurance   45
That my remembrance warrants. [2] Had I not
Four or five women once that tended me?

Prospero

Thou hadst, and more, Miranda. But how is it
That this lives in thy mind? What see'st thou else
past / abyss   In the dark backward° and abysm° of time?   50
anything   If thou rememb'rest aught° ere thou cam'st here,
How thou cam'st here thou mayst. [3]

Miranda

But that I do not.

Prospero

ago   Twelve year since,° Miranda, twelve year since,
Thy father was the Duke of Milan [4] and
with much   A prince of° power.

Miranda

Sir, are not you my father?   55

Prospero

model   Thy mother was a piece° of virtue, and
She said thou wast my daughter. And thy father
Was Duke of Milan, and thou his only heir
And princess no worse issued. [5]

Miranda

O the heavens!
What foul play had we that we came from thence?   60
Or blessèd was 't we did?

1   *teen that I have turned you to*

    **(1) trouble that I have caused you;
(2) trouble that I have now caused
you to recall**

2   *Please you, farther.*

    If you please, go on.

3   *signories*

    **The City-states of the area around
Milan, in Northern Italy**

4   *being all my study*

    I.e., consuming all my attention

5   *transported / And rapt in*

    I.e., carried away by

6   *liberal arts … secret studies*

    **Prospero's academic
achievements encompass both
legitimate learning (*liberal arts*)
and magic (*secret studies*). The
former consisted of the seven
established fields of study—the
trivium (grammar, logic, rhetoric)
and the *quadrivium* (arithmetic,
geometry, music, astronomy)—
whereas the latter are less clear
cut. The audience would be aware
of a dramatic precedent in the
figure of Doctor Faustus, best
known to them from Marlowe's
play, at the end of which the
protagonist is dragged to Hell;
they would therefore be wary of
Prospero's occult learning.**

7   *Being once perfected how to grant suits*

    **Once he (Antonio) mastered the
handling of petitions**

8   *who / To trash for overtopping*

    **Whom to hold in check for being
too ambitious**

9   *new created / The creatures that
were mine*

    **I.e., gained the allegiance of
those who were once loyal to me**

10   *both the key / Of officer and office*

    **The keys to (i.e., control over)
both the government officials
and my administration**

Prospero

>   Both, both, my girl.
> By foul play, as thou say'st, were we heaved thence,

helped But blessedly holp° hither.

Miranda

>   Oh, my heart bleeds

trouble To think o' th' teen° that I have turned you to, [1]

not in Which is from° my remembrance! Please you, farther. [2]   65

Prospero

> My brother and thy uncle, called Antonio—

pay attention to I pray thee, mark° me—that a brother should

deceitful / to you Be so perfidious,° he whom next thyself°

> Of all the world I loved and to him put

management The manage° of my state, as at that time   70

most important Through all the signories [3] it was the first,°

> And Prospero the prime duke, being so reputed
> In dignity, and for the liberal arts
> Without a parallel. Those being all my study, [4]
> The government I cast upon my brother   75

estranged And to my state grew stranger,° being transported

deceitful And rapt in [5] secret studies. [6] Thy false° uncle—

listen to Dost thou attend° me?

Miranda

attentively   Sir, most heedfully.°

Prospero

> Being once perfected how to grant suits, [7]
> How to deny them, who t' advance and who   80
> To trash for overtopping, [8] new created

replaced The creatures that were mine, [9] I say, or changed° 'em

> Or else new formed 'em; having both the key
> Of officer and office, [10] set all hearts i' th' state
> To what tune pleased his ear, that now he was   85

1   *sucked my verdure out on 't*

Sapped the strength from it (i.e.,
***my princely trunk*)**

2   *that which, but by being so retired, /*
    O'erprized all popular rate

(1) those studies that, except for the
fact that they kept me in seclusion,
were more precious than the
populace realized; (2) those studies
that—merely because they made
me seem so remote and secretive—
were deemed more dangerous than
they actually were

3   *my trust, / Like a good parent, did beget*
    of him / A falsehood in its contrary as
    great / As my trust was

Like that of a good parent, my trust
fostered in Antonio a deceit that
was, perversely, as great as my trust
in him had been. "Trust is the
mother of deceit" was proverbial.

4   *lorded*

Made a lord

5   *like one / Who, having into truth by*
    telling of it, / Made such a sinner of his
    memory / To credit his own lie

Like one, who, by repeatedly
telling a lie, tricks his own memory
into believing it true.

6   *out o' th' substitution*

As a result of having substituted
himself for me

7   *prerogative*

I.e., all the powers and privileges
of the office

8   *To have no screen between this part he*
    played / And him he played it for, he
    needs will be / Absolute Milan.

In order to eliminate the distinction
between the role Antonio played
(that of the rightful duke) and the
person whom he played it for
(Prospero), Antonio must himself
become the absolute ruler of Milan.

9   *temporal royalties*

The daily duties of the office of duke

The ivy which had hid my princely trunk
And sucked my verdure out on 't.[1] Thou attend'st not!
Miranda
Oh, good sir, I do.
Prospero
                              I pray thee, mark me.
I, thus neglecting worldly ends, all dedicated

seclusion To closeness° and the bettering of my mind   90
With that which, but by being so retired,
O'erprized all popular rate,[2] in my false brother
Awaked an evil nature; and my trust,
Like a good parent, did beget of him
A falsehood in its contrary as great   95
As my trust was,[3] which had indeed no limit,

without A confidence sans° bound. He being thus lorded,[4]
Not only with what my revenue yielded
But what my power might else exact, like one

sinned against Who, having into° truth by telling of it,   100
Made such a sinner of his memory
To credit his own lie,[5] he did believe
He was indeed the duke, out o' th' substitution[6]

portraying And executing° th' outward face of royalty,
With all prerogative.[7] Hence his ambition growing—   105
Dost thou hear?
Miranda
                              Your tale, sir, would cure deafness.
Prospero

barrier To have no screen° between this part he played
And him he played it for, he needs will be

For me Absolute Milan.[8] Me,° poor man, my library
Was dukedom large enough. Of temporal royalties[9]   110

conspires He thinks me now incapable, confederates°—

1   *So dry he was for sway*

    So thirsty was he for influence

2   *Subject his coronet to his crown*

    **I.e., yield his power to the King of
    Naples's greater authority. Naples
    was a larger and more important
    polity than Milan: it was a kingdom,
    while Milan was only a dukedom. In
    Shakespeare's time, Italy was not yet
    a unified nation; see 1.2.54 and note.**

3   *fair Milan*

    I.e., control over fair Milan

4   *a hint / That wrings mine eyes to 't*

    **An occasion that forces tears from
    my eyes**

So dry he was for sway [1]—wi' th' King of Naples
i.e., the King of Naples To give him° annual tribute, do him homage,
Subject his coronet to his crown, [2] and bend
The dukedom yet unbowed—alas, poor Milan!—   115
To most ignoble stooping.

Miranda

                                O the heavens!

Prospero

terms / outcome Mark his condition° and th' event.° Then tell me
If this might be a brother.

Miranda

                                I should sin
anything but To think but° nobly of my grandmother.
Good wombs have borne bad sons.

Prospero

                                Now the condition.   120
This King of Naples, being an enemy
of long standing / regards To me inveterate,° hearkens° my brother's suit,
Which was that he, in lieu o' th' premises
Of homage and I know not how much tribute,
quickly / uproot Should presently° extirpate° me and mine   125
Out of the dukedom and confer fair Milan [3]
With all the honors on my brother. Whereon,
A treacherous army levied, one midnight
Designated by fate Fated° to th' purpose did Antonio open
The gates of Milan, and, i' th' dead of darkness,   130
away The ministers for th' purpose hurried thence°
Me and thy crying self.

Miranda

                                Alack, for pity!
I, not rememb'ring how I cried out then,
Will cry it o'er again. It is a hint
That wrings mine eyes to 't. [4]

1   *wench*

In Shakespeare's time, this was primarily a term of endearment for a girl or young woman. The word could also be a derogatory term for a woman (as at 1.1.44).

2   *A rotten carcass of a butt*

A rotting skeleton of a tub

3   *hoist us*

Launched us on the sea

4   *Did us but loving wrong*

Wronged us, but without malice (i.e., did us *wrong* by sending us to sea, but *loving* because they drove us to the island)

5   *decked the sea with drops full salt*

Decorated the sea with my own, thoroughly salty drops (i.e., my tears)

6   *which raised in me*

Which refers back to Miranda's smiling *fortitude*.

7   *undergoing stomach*

Strong determination

Prospero

Hear a little further, 135

And then I'll bring thee to the present business

Which now's upon 's, without the which this story

irrelevant Were most impertinent.°

Miranda

Why Wherefore° did they not

That hour destroy us?

Prospero

asked Well demanded,° wench. [1]

dared My tale provokes that question. Dear, they durst° not, 140

So dear the love my people bore me, nor set

A mark so bloody on the business, but

objectives With colors fairer painted their foul ends.°

a few words / ship In few,° they hurried us aboard a bark,°

Bore us some leagues to sea, where they prepared 145

A rotten carcass of a butt, [2] not rigged,

(Possessing) neither Nor° tackle, sail, nor mast. The very rats

left Instinctively have quit° it. There they hoist us, [3]

To cry to th' sea that roared to us, to sigh

To th' winds whose pity, sighing back again, 150

Did us but loving wrong. [4]

Miranda

Alack, what trouble

Was I then to you!

Prospero

cherub; angel Oh, a cherubin°

Thou wast that did preserve me. Thou didst smile,

Infusèd with a fortitude from Heaven,

When I have decked the sea with drops full salt, [5] 155

Under my burden groaned, which raised in me [6]

An undergoing stomach [7] to bear up

Against what should ensue.

1   *steaded much*

     Been very useful

2   *Would I might / But ever see*

     I wish I could someday see

3   *made thee more profit*

     Done you more good

4   *vainer hours*

     Hours spent in emptier pursuits

5   *my zenith*

     I.e., the height of my good fortune

Miranda

How came we ashore?

Prospero

                    By providence divine.

Some food we had and some fresh water that   160

A noble Neapolitan, Gonzalo,

Out of his charity, who being then appointed

scheme   Master of this design,° did give us, with

Rich garments, linens, stuffs, and necessaries,

Which since have steaded much.[1] So, of his gentleness, 165

Knowing I loved my books, he furnished me

From mine own library with volumes that

I prize above my dukedom.

Miranda

                    Would I might

But ever see[2] that man!

Prospero

                  Now I arise.

Sit still and hear the last of our sea-sorrow.   170

Here in this island we arrived, and here

Have I, thy schoolmaster, made thee more profit[3]

Than other princes can that have more time

For vainer hours[4] and tutors not so careful.

Miranda

Heavens thank you for 't! And now, I pray you, sir— 175

For still 'tis beating in my mind—your reason

For raising this sea storm?

Prospero

               Know thus far forth:

By accident most strange, bountiful fortune

(Now my dear lady) hath mine enemies

foreknowledge Brought to this shore. And by my prescience°   180

I find my zenith[5] doth depend upon

1   *If now I court not, but omit*

   If I fail to take advantage (of that star's influence), choosing to ignore it instead

2   *give it way*

   Let it have its way

3   *answer thy best pleasure*

   Do whatever it is you desire

4   *task*

   Used here as a verb; i.e., "command"

5   *quality*

   (1) skills and abilities; (2) followers

6   *to point*

   Down to the last detail

7   *flamed amazement*

   I.e., appeared as fire, so passengers were astonished and frightened

8   *bowsprit*

   Vertical pole that supports a sail's bottom half

9   *distinctly*

   In distinct, individual parts

10 *Jove's*

   Belonging to Jove, King of the Roman gods, equivalent to the Greek Zeus; his primary weapons were lightning bolts.

11 *sight-outrunning*

   Able to run so fast as to be invisible

12 *Neptune*

   God of the sea, in Roman myth; equivalent to the Greek Poseidon

13 *trident*

   The three-pronged spear that was Neptune's traditional weapon

A most auspicious star, whose influence
If now I court not, but omit,[1] my fortunes
Will ever after droop. Here cease more questions.
drowsiness Thou art inclined to sleep. 'Tis a good dulness,° 185
And give it way.[2] I know thou canst not choose.

[**Miranda** *sleeps.*]

[*to* **Ariel**] Come away, servant; come. I am ready now.
Approach, my Ariel; come.

Enter **Ariel**.

Ariel

Venerable; Respected All hail, great master! Grave° sir, hail! I come
To answer thy best pleasure,[3] be 't to fly, 190
To swim, to dive into the fire, to ride
On the curled clouds. To thy strong bidding, task[4]
Ariel and all his quality.[5]

Prospero

Hast thou, spirit,
commanded Performed to point[6] the tempest that I bade° thee?

Ariel

To every article. 195
ship's prow I boarded the King's ship. Now on the beak,°
middle of the ship Now in the waist,° the deck, in every cabin,
divide myself I flamed amazement.[7] Sometime I'd divide°
And burn in many places. On the topmast,
mast crossbars The yards,° and bowsprit[8] would I flame distinctly,[9] 200
Then meet and join. Jove's[10] lightning, the precursors
O' th' dreadful thunder-claps, more momentary
And sight-outrunning[11] were not. The fire and cracks
Of sulphurous roaring the most mighty Neptune[12]
Seem to besiege and make his bold waves tremble, 205
dreaded Yea, his dread° trident[13] shake.

1   *Not a soul / But felt*

    There wasn't a soul that didn't feel

2   *played / Some tricks of desperation*

    **Expressed their desperation in
    some way**

3   *Then all afire with me*

    **The lack of Folio punctuation after
    me suggests somewhat improbably
    that it is Ferdinand who is *all afire*
    along with Ariel.**

4   *sustaining garments*

    **The sailors' clothing may have kept
    them afloat**

5   *in this sad knot*

    **I.e., crossed, a conventional sign of
    melancholy or sorrow**

Prospero

My brave spirit!

tumult   Who was so firm, so constant, that this coil°

Would not infect his reason?

Ariel

Not a soul

But felt [1] a fever of the mad and played

Some tricks of desperation. [2] All but mariners   210

left   Plunged in the foaming brine and quit° the vessel,

Then all afire with me. [3] The King's son, Ferdinand,

on end   With hair up-staring°—then like reeds, not hair—

Was the first man that leaped, cried, "Hell is empty,

And all the devils are here."

Prospero

Why, that's my spirit!   215

near   But was not this nigh° shore?

Ariel

Close by, my master.

Prospero

But are they, Ariel, safe?

Ariel

Not a hair perished.

On their sustaining garments [4] not a blemish,

commanded   But fresher than before. And, as thou bad'st° me,

groups   In troops° I have dispersed them 'bout the isle.   220

The King's son have I landed by himself,

Whom I left cooling of the air with sighs

corner   In an odd angle° of the isle, and sitting,

His arms in this sad knot. [5]

Prospero

Of the King's ship,

The mariners, say how thou hast disposed   225

And all the rest o' th' fleet.

1   *still-vexed*

Constantly disturbed by storms

2   *Bermudas*

The islands of Bermuda, named
after their Spanish "discoverer"
Juan de Bermúdez, were thought
to be both magical and dangerous,
a reputation still alive and well
now through the mystery of the
"Bermuda triangle." This
reference, along with the echoes
elsewhere in the play of an
epistolary account by William
Strachey of a shipwreck in 1609 on
Bermuda, has led to *The Tempest*'s
identification as a "New World"
play and its association, both in
performance and in criticism, with
questions of colonialism. Strachey
described Bermuda as "dangerous
and dreaded," notable for
"tempests" and "thunders." *The
Bermudas* was also the name given
to a part of London known as a safe
haven for outlaws and prostitutes,
so while looking away from home
the reference also glances inward.

3   *with a charm joined to their suffered labor*

With a magic spell that will
intensify the exhaustion they
already feel from their hard labor

4   *glasses*

Hourglasses (i.e., hours)

5   *performed me*

Done for me

6   *the time be out*

The prescribed period has been
completed

Ariel

                                        Safely in harbor

bay   Is the King's ship; in the deep nook° where once

            Thou called'st me up at midnight to fetch dew

            From the still-vexed [1] Bermudas, [2] there she's hid,

deck   The mariners all under hatches° stowed,   230

            Who, with a charm joined to their suffered labor, [3]

as for   I have left asleep. And for° the rest o' th' fleet

            Which I dispersed, they all have met again

sea   And are upon the Mediterranean float°

            Bound sadly home for Naples,   235

wrecked   Supposing that they saw the King's ship wracked°

            And his great person perish.

Prospero

duty   Ariel, thy charge°

            Exactly is performed. But there's more work.

            What is the time o' th' day?

Ariel

noon   Past the mid-season.°

Prospero

            At least two glasses. [4] The time 'twixt six and now   240

            Must by us both be spent most preciously.

Ariel

tasks   Is there more toil? Since thou dost give me pains,°

remind   Let me remember° thee what thou hast promised,

            Which is not yet performed me. [5]

Prospero

                                        How now? Moody?

            What is 't thou canst demand?

Ariel

                                        My liberty.   245

Prospero

            Before the time be out? [6] No more!

1   *or . . . or*
    Either . . . or

2   *bate me*
    I.e., reduce my sentence by

3   *think'st it much to*
    Think you do me great service
    when you

4   *the ooze / Of the salt deep*
    The ocean's muddy floor

5   *who with age and envy / Was grown into
    a hoop*
    Sycorax's back became hunched
    over with age, her body deformed
    with the force of her own malice
    (*envy*).

6   *witch Sycorax*
    The most likely origins of Sycorax's
    name are the Greek for "sow" (*sus*)
    and for "raven" (*corax*), both of
    which have been associated with
    witchcraft. Caliban associates his
    mother with a *raven's feather* at
    1.2.323. Her character appears to
    derive from the description in
    Ovid's *Metamorphoses*, Book Seven,
    of the murderous witch Medea,
    who was known as the "Scythian
    raven" and who, along with the
    sorceress Circe, who turns men
    into pigs in Homer's *Odyssey*, is
    associated with Colchis, where a
    tribe called the Coraxi lived. Like
    most witches at this time, Sycorax
    is imagined as an ancient and
    malicious woman, bent double
    with age. Sycorax was long dead
    before Prospero arrived on the
    island, but she has a considerable
    hold over his imagination as his
    negative female counterpart whose
    island-educated son is in turn the
    polar opposite of Miranda.

Ariel

pray you   I prithee°

Remember I have done thee worthy service,

Told thee no lies, made thee no mistakings, served

Without or grudge or ¹ grumblings. Thou did promise

To bate me ² a full year.

Prospero

                                Dost thou forget   250

From what a torment I did free thee?

Ariel

                                        No.

Prospero

Thou dost, and think'st it much to ³ tread the ooze

Of the salt deep, ⁴

To run upon the sharp wind of the north,

To do me business in the veins o' th' earth   255

hardened   When it is baked° with frost.

Ariel

                                        I do not, sir.

Prospero

Thou liest, malignant thing! Hast thou forgot

The foul witch Sycorax, who with age and envy

Was grown into a hoop? ⁵ Hast thou forgot her?

Ariel

No, sir.

Prospero

        Thou hast. Where was she born? Speak. Tell me.   260

Ariel

Sir, in Algiers.

Prospero

            Oh, was she so? I must

Once in a month recount what thou hast been,

Which thou forget'st. This damned witch Sycorax, ⁶

1   *For one thing she did / They would not
    take her life.*

The *one thing* has often been
debated, but Sycorax's life was
seemingly spared because she was
pregnant (with Caliban) at the time
of her banishment, as the
conventions of many European
countries allowed. Pregnant
women were held to be *blue-eyed*
(line 269), i.e., marked by a bluish
tinge to the eyelid, though, as Leah
Marcus notes, the image may be
literal, unsettling the assumptions
of some 19th-century critics who
would deny an Algerian what they
considered a superior Anglo-saxon
characteristic.

2   *To act her earthy and abhorred
    commands*

To perform the bestial and hated
acts she demanded

3   *unmitigable*

Incapable of being satisfied

4   *As fast as mill wheels strike*

As often as the blades of a mill
wheel hit the water

5   *litter*

Give birth to. The term is usually
used in reference to animals.

6   *A freckled whelp, hag-born*

A spotted puppy, born of a witch

7   *I say so*

Just as I said

8   *Caliban*

Critics argue over the origin and
meaning of Caliban's name, and
various options have been
suggested. The most likely is that it
is a near anagram of *cannibal*:
people who eat human flesh are
mentioned by Shakespeare in
Othello, and lurid drawings of the
alleged cannibalism of New World
natives circulated in the 16th and
17th centuries. The word *cannibal* in
turn derives from "Carib," a name
used for various New World
peoples, especially those of the
islands in what became known as
the Caribbean. In the 1623 Folio's
list of roles, Caliban is described as
a "savage and deformed slave,"
savage meaning uncivilized,
deformed implying moral as well as
physical defects, and *slave*
suggesting that his nature is such
that he needs inevitably to be kept
under control—as if servitude is a
natural state for him, an
imputation he resists fiercely,
especially at 1.2.332–345.

9   *penetrate the breasts*

Touched the hearts

For mischiefs manifold and sorceries terrible
To enter human hearing, from Argier,   265
Thou know'st, was banished. For one thing she did
They would not take her life. [1] Is not this true?

Ariel

Ay, sir.

Prospero

witch   This blue-eyed hag° was hither brought with child
And here was left by th' sailors. Thou, my slave,   270
As thou report'st thyself, was then her servant,
because / were   And, for° thou wast° a spirit too delicate
To act her earthy and abhorred commands, [2]
behests; orders   Refusing her grand hests,° she did confine thee,
agents   By help of her more potent ministers°   275
And in her most unmitigable [3] rage,
split   Into a cloven° pine, within which rift
Imprisoned thou didst painfully remain
A dozen years—within which space she died
And left thee there, where thou didst vent thy groans   280
As fast as mill wheels strike. [4] Then was this island—
Except   Save° for the son that she did litter [5] here,
A freckled whelp, hag-born [6]—not honored with
A human shape.

Ariel

                    Yes, Caliban her son.

Prospero

Dull thing, I say so: [7] he, that Caliban [8]   285
Whom now I keep in service. Thou best know'st
What torment I did find thee in. Thy groans
Did make wolves howl and penetrate the breasts [9]
Of ever angry bears. It was a torment
To lay upon the damned, which Sycorax   290
Could not again undo. It was mine art,

1   *make thyself like*

    Take on the guise of

2   *invisible*

    Prospero sends Ariel away to
    metamorphose into the image of a
    sea nymph and become invisible to
    all but the two of them. *Go take this
    shape* perhaps implies that Prospero
    hands him a garment of some kind;
    if so, that means that each of the
    preexisting inhabitants of the island
    has a distinctive item of clothing—
    Caliban his *gaberdine*, Ariel his
    shape—just as Prospero himself has
    his magic cloak. Theater manager
    Philip Henslowe, one of
    Shakespeare's contemporaries,
    records "a robe for to go invisible" as
    one of the Admiral's Men's props,
    which suggests a convention the
    audience would understand.
    Presumably the garment, if that is
    what it is, is sea colored.

3   *put / Heaviness in me*

    Made me heavy with sleep

open   When I arrived and heard thee, that made gape°
The pine and let thee out.

Ariel

                  I thank thee, master.

Prospero

complain   If thou more murmur'st,° I will rend an oak
And peg thee in his knotty entrails till   295
Thou hast howled away twelve winters.

Ariel

                     Pardon, master.

responsive   I will be correspondent° to command
And do my spiriting gently.

Prospero

                Do so,
And after two days I will discharge thee.

Ariel

That's my noble master!   300
What shall I do? Say, what? What shall I do?

Prospero

Go make thyself like[1] a nymph o' th' sea.
Be subject to no sight but thine and mine, invisible[2]
To every eyeball else. Go take this shape
And hither come in 't. Go hence with diligence!   305

                     [**Ariel**] *exits.*

[*to* **Miranda**] Awake, dear heart, awake! Thou hast slept
    well.
Awake!

Miranda

           [*waking*] The strangeness of your story put
Heaviness in me.[3]

Prospero

              Shake it off. Come on.

1   *serves in offices*

    Performs duties

2   *When?*

    **An expression of impatience
    ("Come on!")**

3   like

    In the shape of

4   *dam*

    Mother (usually reserved for animals)

We'll visit Caliban, my slave who never
Yields us kind answer.

Miranda

                              'Tis a villain, sir,   310

I do not love to look on.

Prospero

                              But, as 'tis,

get along without   We cannot miss° him. He does make our fire,
Fetch in our wood, and serves in offices[1]
That profit us.—What, ho! Slave! Caliban!
Thou earth, thou! Speak.

Caliban

                       [_within_] There's wood enough within. 315

Prospero

Come forth, I say! There's other business for thee.
Come, thou tortoise! When?[2]

       Enter **Ariel**, _like[3] a water nymph._

ingenious Fine apparition! My quaint° Ariel,
Hark in thine ear. [_whispers to_ **Ariel**]

Ariel

                      My lord, it shall be done.   _He exits._

Prospero

Thou poisonous slave, got by the devil himself   320
Upon thy wicked dam,[4] come forth!

       Enter **Caliban**.

Caliban

As wicked dew as e'er my mother brushed

marsh With raven's feather from unwholesome fen°

1   *southwest*

Southwest winds are damp and humid and were assumed to carry disease.

2   *Side-stitches that shall pen thy breath up*

Pains in your sides that will make you short of breath

3   *Urchins*

Hedgehogs; or, more likely here, goblins taking the shape of hedgehogs

4   *at vast of night that they may work / All exercise on thee*

During the desolate period of night in which they work to harass you in all manner of ways

5   *pinched / As thick as honeycomb*

I.e., pinched as much as the cells of the honeycomb (an image deriving from the belief that bees pinch the comb into shape)

6   *Than bees that made 'em*

Than the (sting of) bees that made them (the honeycomb cells)

7   *Water with berries in 't*

I.e., cedar berries and water, which, according to Strachey (one of Shakespeare's sources) "made a kind of pleasant drink"

8   *how / To name the bigger light and how the less*

What to call the sun, and what to call the moon (echoing Genesis 1:16, which describes how "God made the two great lights—the greater light to rule the day and the lesser light to rule the night")

9   *sty me*

Confine me (like a pig in a *sty*)

10   *stripes may move*

Whipping may influence

Drop on you both! A southwest[1] blow on ye
And blister you all o'er! 325
Prospero
For this, be sure, tonight thou shalt have cramps,
Side-stitches that shall pen thy breath up.[2] Urchins[3]
Come forth Shall forth° at vast of night that they may work
All exercise on thee.[4] Thou shalt be pinched
As thick as honeycomb,[5] each pinch more stinging 330
Than bees that made 'em.[6]
Caliban
                                        I must eat my dinner.
This island's mine, by Sycorax my mother,
Which thou tak'st from me. When thou cam'st first,
stroked Thou strok'st° me and made much of me, wouldst give me
Water with berries in 't,[7] and teach me how 335
To name the bigger light and how the less,[8]
That burn by day and night. And then I loved thee
aspects And showed thee all the qualities° o' th' isle:
The fresh springs, brine pits, barren place and fertile.
Cursed be I that did so! All the charms 340
Of Sycorax—toads, beetles, bats—light on you,
For I am all the subjects that you have,
Which first was mine own king. And here you sty me[9]
In this hard rock, whiles you do keep from me
The rest o' th' island.
Prospero
                                        Thou most lying slave, 345
treated Whom stripes may move,[10] not kindness! I have used° thee,
Filth as thou art, with humane care, and lodged thee
In mine own cell, till thou didst seek to violate
The honor of my child.
Caliban
Oh ho, oh ho! Would 't had been done! 350

1   *I had peopled else*

Otherwise I would have populated

2   *Which any print of goodness wilt
    not take*

Who cannot be imprinted with
goodness (i.e., influenced to be
good)

3   *vile race*

The word *race* did not in
Shakespeare's day mean exactly
what it means to us: it did not
necessarily imply ethnicity but
rather, in *OED*'s phrasing, "natural
or inherited disposition."
Nevertheless, in the context of
Sycorax's Algerian origins, it is hard
not to see in Miranda's deep
distaste for Caliban an instance of
what we would describe as racism.

4   *my profit on 't*

The benefit I've gotten from it

5   *The red plague rid you / For learning me*

Let the plague that leaves red sores
on your body destroy you for
teaching me

6   *and be quick, thou 'rt best, / To answer
    other business*

And hurry, if you know what's good
for you, to perform whatever else is
asked of you

7   *rack thee with old cramps*

I.e., wrack your body with the pains
of old age

8   *Setebos*

In Antonio Pigafetta's account of
Magellan's voyages (first published in
English in 1555), the Patagonians are
said to worship a "great devil *Setebos*."

Thou didst prevent me. I had peopled else [1]
This isle with Calibans.

Miranda

                    Abhorrèd slave,
Which any print of goodness wilt not take, [2]

evil   Being capable of all ill!° I pitied thee,

Took pains to make thee speak, taught thee each hour   *355*
One thing or other. When thou didst not, savage,
Know thine own meaning, but wouldst gabble like
A thing most brutish, I endowed thy purposes
With words that made them known. But thy vile race, [3]
Though thou didst learn, had that in 't which good
    natures   *360*
Could not abide to be with. Therefore wast thou
Deservedly confined into this rock,

worse   Who hadst deserved more° than a prison.

Caliban

You taught me language, and my profit on 't [4]
Is I know how to curse. The red plague rid you   *365*
For learning me [5] your language!

Prospero

Witch's child / begone   Hag-seed,° hence!°
Fetch us in fuel, and be quick, thou 'rt best,

i.e., malicious creature   To answer other business. [6] Shrug'st thou, malice?°
If thou neglect'st or dost unwillingly
What I command, I'll rack thee with old cramps, [7]   *370*
Fill all thy bones with aches, make thee roar

So that   That° beasts shall tremble at thy din.

Caliban

                          No, pray thee.
[*aside*] I must obey. His art is of such power
It would control my dam's god, Setebos, [8]

slave   And make a vassal° of him.

1   *and kissed / The wild waves whist*

    **And kissed the unruly waves until
    they have grown silent**

2   *Foot it featly*

    Dance with agility

3   *bear / The burden*

    I.e., sing the chorus

4   burden dispersedly

    ***Dispersedly* means either the spirits
    sing the song from different
    positions in the theater or that they
    sing not in unison.**

5   *waits upon*

    Serves, like a servant or courtier

6   *Allaying both their fury and my passion /
    With its sweet air*

    **Calming both the waters' turbulence
    and my own suffering with its sweet
    melody**

Prospero

So, slave; hence!   375

Caliban *exits.*

Enter **Ferdinand** *and* **Ariel**, *invisible, playing and singing.*

Ariel

[*sings*] Come unto these yellow sands
And then take hands;
Courtsied when you have and kissed
The wild waves whist; [1]
Foot it featly [2] here and there,   380
And, sweet sprites, bear
The burden. [3] Hark, hark!

Spirits

(*burden dispersedly,* [4] [*within*]) Bow-wow!

Ariel

The watch-dogs bark!

Spirits

[*within*] Bow-wow.   385

Ariel

Hark, hark! I hear
rooster   The strain of strutting chanticleer°
Cry, "Cock-a-diddle-dow."

Ferdinand

Where should this music be? I' th' air or th' earth?
surely   It sounds no more, and sure° it waits upon [5]   390
Some god o' th' island. Sitting on a bank,
shipwreck   Weeping again the King my father's wrack,°
This music crept by me upon the waters,
Allaying both their fury and my passion
With its sweet air. [6] Thence I have followed it,   395
Or it hath drawn me rather. But 'tis gone.

1   *Full fathom five*

   Fully five fathoms below. A *fathom*
   is about two yards.

2   *But doth suffer*

   Except what undergoes

3   *ring his knell*

   Sound the death knell for him

4   *mortal business*

   I.e., work of human beings

5   *The fringèd curtains of thine eye advance*

   I.e., lift your eyelids (which are
   ***fringed* with eyelashes)**

6   *but he's something stained / With grief*
   (that's beauty's canker) thou mightst call
   him / A goodly person

   Except for the fact that he's somewhat
   touched by grief, which is a worm that
   feeds on the flower of beauty, you
   could call him a handsome man

No, it begins again.

Ariel

[*sings*] Full fathom five [1] thy father lies.

Of his bones are coral made;

Those are pearls that were his eyes: 400

Nothing of him that doth fade

But doth suffer [2] a sea-change

Into something rich and strange.

Sea-nymphs hourly ring his knell. [3]

Spirits

[*within*] Ding-dong.   405

Ariel

Hark! Now I hear them.

Spirits

                                    [*within*] Ding-dong, bell.

Ferdinand

commemorate   The ditty does remember° my drowned father.

This is no mortal business, [4] nor no sound

owns   That the earth owes.° I hear it now above me.

Prospero

[*to* **Miranda**] The fringèd curtains of thine eye advance [5]   410

yonder   And say what thou see'st yond.°

Miranda

                                    What is 't? A spirit?

Lord, how it looks about! Believe me, sir,

handsome   It carries a brave° form. But 'tis a spirit.

Prospero

No, wench. It eats and sleeps and hath such senses

fine gentleman   As we have, such. This gallant° which thou see'st   415

Was in the wrack, and, but he's something stained

With grief (that's beauty's canker) thou mightst call him

A goodly person. [6] He hath lost his fellows

wanders   And strays° about to find 'em.

1   *nothing natural / I ever saw so noble*

I never saw a natural creature who looked so noble

2   *It goes on, I see, / As my soul prompts it.*

It's transpiring, I see, just as I'd hoped.

3   *Vouchsafe my prayer / May know*

Grant my prayer that I may know

4   *And that you will some good instruction give / How I may bear me*

And that you will instruct me how I should conduct myself

5   *wonder*

Miracle (punning on Miranda's name, which derives from the Latin verb "to wonder")

6   *maid*

Three possible meanings, all in play: (1) a human woman as opposed to a goddess; (2) a young, unmarried woman; (3) a virgin

7   *the best of them that speak this speech*

I.e., the highest in rank among those who speak Italian. Believing his father dead in the shipwreck, Ferdinand assumes he is now the King of Naples.

8   *A single thing*

(1) the King himself; (2) an isolated and vulnerable creature; and perhaps (3) a bachelor

9   *He does hear me, / And that he does I weep.*

He hears me, and for that I weep.

10   *never since at ebb*

Flowing with tears ever since (*ebb* = low tide)

Miranda

                              I might call him
A thing divine, for nothing natural   420
I ever saw so noble. [1]

Prospero

                    [*aside*] It goes on, I see,
As my soul prompts it. [2]—Spirit, fine spirit! I'll free thee
Within two days for this.

Ferdinand

                    [*seeing* **Miranda**] Most sure, the goddess
On whom these airs° attend! Vouchsafe my prayer

songs

May know [3] if you remain° upon this island,   425

dwell

And that you will some good instruction give
How I may bear me [4] here. My prime request,
Which I do last pronounce, is—O you wonder! [5]—
If you be maid [6] or no?

Miranda

                              No wonder, sir,
But certainly a maid.

Ferdinand

                              My language? Heavens,   430
I am the best of them that speak this speech, [7]
Were I but where 'tis spoken.

Prospero

                              How? The best?
What wert thou if the King of Naples heard thee?

Ferdinand

A single thing, [8] as I am now, that wonders°

is amazed

To hear thee speak of Naples. He does hear me,   435

the King of Naples

And that he does I weep. [9] Myself am Naples,°
Who with mine eyes, never since at ebb, [10] beheld

destroyed

The King my father wracked.°

1   *his brave son*

This phrase parallels *The Duke of Milan
/ And his more braver daughter* but
presents a problem, since there is no
other mention in the play of Antonio
having a son. The usual assumption
is that Shakespeare originally
planned to incorporate an
additional character as a balance for
Miranda (as Dryden and Davenant
did in a different way in their
adaptation) but decided against it
and simply forgot to erase this
reference. David Scott Kastan
observes that Prospero's dynastic
plan in marrying Miranda to
Ferdinand would in any case ensure
the erasure of Antonio's line of
succession, so there is an ironic
thematic underpinning to this
textual crux.

2   *changed eyes*

Exchanged loving glances (and,
presumably, fallen in love)

3   *not gone forth*

Not bestowed elsewhere

4   *but this swift business / I must uneasy
make, lest too light winning / Make the
prize light*

But I must complicate this swift
business (of falling in love), lest
the prize become devalued, having
been won so easily

5   *Thou dost here usurp / The name thou
ow'st not*

You have wrongfully taken on a
name that does not belong to you

Miranda

Alack, for mercy!

Ferdinand

Yes, faith, and all his lords—the Duke of Milan

two of them   And his brave son [1] being twain.°

Prospero

[*aside*] The Duke of Milan   440

challenge   And his more braver daughter could control° thee

If now 'twere fit to do 't! At the first sight

They have changed eyes. [2]—Delicate Ariel,

I'll set thee free for this.

[*to **Ferdinand**] A word, good sir;

I fear you have done yourself some wrong. A word.   445

Miranda

[*aside*] Why speaks my father so ungently? This

Is the third man that e'er I saw, the first

That e'er I sighed for. Pity move my father

To be inclined my way!

Ferdinand

[*to **Miranda**] Oh, if a virgin,

And your affection not gone forth, [3] I'll make you   450

The queen of Naples.

Prospero

Quiet   Soft,° sir! One word more.

[*aside*] They are both in either's powers; but this swift business

I must uneasy make, lest too light winning

Make the prize light. [4] [*to **Ferdinand**] One word more.

I charge thee

pay attention to   That thou attend° me. Thou dost here usurp   455

owns   The name thou ow'st° not [5] and hast put thyself

Upon this island as a spy to win it

From me, the lord on 't.

1　*temple*

I.e., Ferdinand's body

2　*husks / Wherein the acorn cradled*

Empty acorn shells

3　charmed from moving

Is frozen in place by a magic charm

4　*Make not too rash a trial of him*

Do not test him too recklessly

5　*My foot my tutor*

Prospero draws on the proverb "Do not make the foot the head" as he asserts his authority over his child.

6　*Come from thy ward*

I.e., put down your arms. In fencing, the *ward* is a defensive stance.

Ferdinand

No, as I am a man!

Miranda

There's nothing ill can dwell in such a temple. [1]

If the ill spirit have so fair a house,   460

Good things will strive to dwell with 't.

Prospero

[*to* **Ferdinand**] Follow me.

—Speak not you for him. He's a traitor.—Come;

I'll manacle thy neck and feet together.

Sea-water shalt thou drink. Thy food shall be

The fresh-brook mussels, withered roots, and husks   465

Wherein the acorn cradled. [2] Follow.

Ferdinand

No.

treatment I will resist such entertainment° till

Mine enemy has more power.

[**Ferdinand**] *draws* [*his sword*] *and is charmed from moving.* [3]

Miranda

O dear father,

Make not too rash a trial of him, [4] for

threatening He's gentle and not fearful.°

Prospero

What? I say,   470

subordinate My foot° my tutor? [5]—Put thy sword up, traitor,

Who mak'st a show but dar'st not strike, thy conscience

Is so possessed with guilt. Come from thy ward, [6]

For I can here disarm thee with this stick

And make thy weapon drop.

Miranda

I beg Beseech° you, father.   475

1   *such shapes as he*

    Men shaped like him (i.e., as
    attractive as him)

2   *but light*

    Merely trifles

Prospero

Hence! Hang not on my garments.

Miranda

Sir, have pity;

guarantee I'll be his surety.°

Prospero

Silence! One word more

Shall make me chide thee, if not hate thee. What,

An advocate for an imposter! Hush,

Thou think'st there is no more such shapes as he, [1]   480

Having seen but him and Caliban. Foolish wench,

In comparison to To° th' most of men this is a Caliban

And they to him are angels.

Miranda

My affections

Are then most humble. I have no ambition

better-looking To see a goodlier° man.

Prospero

[*to* **Ferdinand**] Come on. Obey.   485

sinews Thy nerves° are in their infancy again

And have no vigor in them.

Ferdinand

So they are.

My spirits, as in a dream, are all bound up.

My father's loss, the weakness which I feel,

and The wrack of all my friends, nor° this man's threats,   490

To whom I am subdued, are but light [2] to me,

Might I but through my prison once a day

Behold this maid. All corners else o' th' earth

i.e., free people Let liberty° make use of. Space enough

Have I in such a prison.

Prospero

[*aside*] It works.

1   *To th' syllable*

In every detail

[*to* **Ferdinand**] Come on.   *495*

—Thou hast done well, fine Ariel!

           [*to* **Ferdinand**] Follow me.

do for   [*to* **Ariel**] Hark what thou else shalt do° me.

Miranda

                  [*to* **Ferdinand**] Be of comfort;

My father's of a better nature, sir,

not typical Than he appears by speech. This is unwonted°

Which now came from him.

Prospero

                [*to* **Ariel**] Thou shalt be free *500*

until then As mountain winds, but then° exactly do

All points of my command.

Ariel

          To th' syllable. ¹

Prospero

[*to* **Ferdinand**] Come; follow. [*to* **Miranda**] Speak not

   for him.   *They exit.*

1 *Our hint of woe / Is common.*

(1) our occasion for grief is common (i.e., many people have suffered in this fashion); (2) this is just a hint of calamity, not a full-fledged catastrophe.

2 *like cold porridge*

As if it were cold pease porridge. Sebastian makes a pun on Alonso's *peace*, peas being a common ingredient in porridge.

3 *The visitor will not give him o'er so.*

The visitor (Gonzalo) will not leave the King to his grief, or perhaps "will not abandon him." A *visitor* is a member of the parish who provides solace to the sick.

4 *One. Tell.*

I.e., it is one o'clock. Keep counting.

Act 2, Scene 1

Enter **Alonso**, **Sebastian**, **Antonio**, **Gonzalo**, **Adrian**,
Francisco, *and others.*

Gonzalo

I beg   [*to* **Alonso**] Beseech° you, sir, be merry. You have
      cause,

      So have we all, of joy, for our escape

greater than   Is much beyond° our loss. Our hint of woe

      Is common.[1] Every day some sailor's wife,

i.e., merchant ship   The masters of some merchant,° and the merchant   5

Except   Have just our theme of woe. But° for the miracle—

      I mean our preservation—few in millions

      Can speak like us. Then wisely, good sir, weigh

against   Our sorrow with° our comfort.

Alonso

                           Prithee, peace.

Sebastian

[*to* **Antonio**] He receives comfort like cold porridge.[2]   10

Antonio

[*to* **Sebastian**] The visitor will not give him o'er so.[3]

Sebastian

Look, he's winding up the watch of his wit. By and by it
will strike.

Gonzalo

[*to* **Alonso**] Sir,—

Sebastian

[*to* **Antonio**] One. Tell.[4]   15

Gonzalo

When every grief is entertained that's offered,
Comes to th' entertainer—

Sebastian

A dollar.

1   *Dolor*

   Sorrow (but Gonzalo puns on
   Sebastian's *dollar*, the English name
   for the German "Thaler," a silver coin)

2   *The wager? / A laughter*

   I.e., what do I get if I win the bet? A
   good laugh (though *laughter* might
   also refer to the set of eggs laid by a
   hen; picking up the earlier
   references to *cock* and *cockerel*.)

Gonzalo

Dolor[1] comes to him, indeed. You have spoken truer

intended than you purposed.°   20

Sebastian

more seriously You have taken it wiselier° than I meant you should.

Gonzalo

[*to* **Alonso**] Therefore, my lord—

Antonio

Fie, what a spendthrift is he of his tongue!

Alonso

[*to* **Gonzalo**] I prithee, spare.

Gonzalo

Well, I have done. But yet—   25

Sebastian

[*to* **Antonio**] He will be talking.

Antonio

[*to* **Sebastian**] Which, of he or Adrian, for a good
wager, first begins to crow?

Sebastian

rooster (i.e., Gonzalo) [*to* **Antonio**] The old cock.°

Antonio

young fowl (i.e., Adrian) [*to* **Sebastian**] The cockerel.°   30

Sebastian

[*to* **Antonio**] Done. The wager?

Antonio

[*to* **Sebastian**] A laughter.[2]

Sebastian

[*to* **Antonio**] A match!

Adrian

deserted [*to* **Gonzalo**] Though this island seem to be desert°—

Antonio

Ha, ha, ha!   35

1   *He could not miss 't.*

    I.e., it was inevitable he would say

2   *Temperance*

    **Antonio puns on the fact that
    Temperance was a common
    female name.**

Sebastian

[*to* **Antonio**] So; you're paid.

Adrian

Uninhabitable and almost inaccessible—

Sebastian

[*to* **Antonio**] Yet—

Adrian

Yet—

Antonio

[*to* **Sebastian**] He could not miss 't. [1]   40

Adrian

refined   It must needs be of subtle,° tender, and delicate

climate   temperance.°

Antonio

sensual   [*to* **Sebastian**] Temperance [2] was a delicate° wench.

Sebastian

cunning person   [*to* **Antonio**] Ay, and a subtle,° as he most learnedly delivered.

Adrian

The air breathes upon us here most sweetly.   45

Sebastian

[*to* **Antonio**] As if it had lungs, and rotten ones.

Antonio

marsh   [*to* **Sebastian**] Or as 'twere perfumed by a fen.°

Gonzalo

Here is everything advantageous to life.

Antonio

except for   [*to* **Sebastian**] True; save° means to live.

Sebastian

[*to* **Antonio**] Of that there's none, or little.   50

Gonzalo

healthy   How lush and lusty° the grass looks! How green!

Antonio

yellow   The ground indeed is tawny.°

1 *pocket up*

Suppress

2 *Dido's*

Dido was a legendary queen of
Carthage. Known principally from
Virgil's *Aeneid*, she was the widow
of Sychaeus and became Aeneas's
tragic lover, killing herself when he
left her. The quips that follow
respond to this history, as well as
the debate over whether or not the
modern Tunis was built on the
remains of the ancient Carthage.

Sebastian

spot With an eye° of green in 't.

Antonio

[*to* **Sebastian**] He misses not much.

Sebastian

[*to* **Antonio**] No, he doth but mistake the truth totally.   55

Gonzalo

But the rarity of it is—which is indeed almost beyond

belief credit°—

Sebastian

supposed [*to* **Antonio**] As many vouched° rarities are.

Gonzalo

That our garments, being, as they were, drenched in

the sea, hold notwithstanding their freshness and   60

gloss, being rather new-dyed than stained with salt

water.

Antonio

[*to* **Sebastian**] If but one of his pockets could speak,

would it not say he lies?

Sebastian

[*to* **Antonio**] Ay, or very falsely pocket up[1] his report.   65

Gonzalo

Methinks our garments are now as fresh as when we

put them on first in Afric, at the marriage of the King's

fair daughter Claribel to the King of Tunis.

Sebastian

'Twas a sweet marriage, and we prosper well in our

return.   70

Adrian

Tunis was never graced before with such a paragon to

their queen.

Gonzalo

Not since widow Dido's[2] time.

1   *A pox o' that!*

     A plague on that notion!

2   *widower Aenas*

     Aeneas was in fact a widower, his
     wife, Creusa, dying in the
     destruction of Troy.

3   *This Tunis, sir, was Carthage.*

     Gonzalo is incorrect—Tunis and
     Carthage were not the same city,
     but after Carthage was destroyed in
     146 B.C., Tunis replaced it as the
     chief city of the region. The
     conjunction of Tunis, a
     contemporary Muslim city, with
     Carthage, the classical city-state
     that was Rome's main rival in the
     days of the Republic, sets up
     resonances that persist
     throughout the play, associating
     Rome's imperial achievements
     negatively with those of the
     Ottoman Empire of Shakespeare's
     day while at the same time,
     through Sebastian and Antonio's
     skepticism, ducking that
     association. Spain had repeatedly
     attempted to invade Tunis in the
     16th century, suggesting its status
     as a threat to Christian civilization
     (Rome had successfully attacked
     and destroyed Carthage after a
     lengthy struggle). This makes
     apparent the reasons for the
     discomfort the courtiers feel about
     Alonso's marrying his daughter
     Claribel to the King of Tunis, a
     discomfort not only based

on the fear of miscegenation but
also on a sense of the threat
located on the southern and
eastern bounds of the
Mediterranean.

4   *miraculous harp*

     An allusion to the Greek myth of
     Amphion, who raised the city of
     Thebes by playing his harp.
     Sebastian implies that Gonzalo has
     similarly *raised* (i.e., invented) the city
     of Carthage in a place where it never
     existed.

Antonio

[*to* **Sebastian**] Widow? A pox o' that![1] How came that
"widow" in? Widow Dido! 75

Sebastian

[*to* **Antonio**] What if he had said "widower Aeneas"[2]
too? Good lord, how you take it!

Adrian

[*to* **Gonzalo**] "Widow Dido," said you? You make me
ponder   study° of that. She was of Carthage, not of Tunis.

Gonzalo

This Tunis, sir, was Carthage.[3] 80

Adrian

Carthage?

Gonzalo

I assure you, Carthage.

Antonio

[*to* **Sebastian**] His word is more than the miraculous harp.[4]

Sebastian

[*to* **Antonio**] He hath raised the wall and houses too.

Antonio

What impossible matter will he make easy next? 85

Sebastian

I think he will carry this island home in his pocket and
give it his son for an apple.

Antonio

And, sowing the kernels of it in the sea, bring forth
more islands.

Gonzalo

[*to* **Adrian**] Ay. 90

Antonio

[*to* **Sebastian**] Why, in good time.

Gonzalo

[*to* **Alonso**] Sir, we were talking that our garments

1   *the marriage of your daughter*

The second of the recorded early
performances of the play took
place in a context that would add
some uncomfortable resonances
to the courtiers' regret about the
marriage of Claribel and the King
of Tunis. In 1613 several of
Shakespeare's plays, including *The
Tempest*, were put on as part of the
celebrations for the wedding of
James I's daughter Elizabeth to
Frederick, the Elector Palatine,
who was the most powerful
Protestant ruler in what we would
now call Germany. James's dynastic
plan was to marry his children to
both Roman Catholic and
Protestant royals and thus oblige
the warring nations to become
peaceful. James never succeeded
in making a Spanish match for his
son, and even Frederick was ousted
from Bohemia, where he had been
proclaimed monarch, by Habsburg
forces. The royal couple spent the
rest of their lives in exile. James
never again saw his daughter after
the wedding.

2   *against / The stomach of my sense*

I.e., in spite of the fact I am in no
mood for this (the image is of force
feeding)

3   *that o'er his wave-worn basis bowed*

Which bent down over its eroded
base

seem now as fresh as when we were at Tunis at the
marriage of your daughter, [1] who is now Queen.

Antonio

And the rarest that e'er came there.   95

Sebastian

Except for Bate,° I beseech you, widow Dido.

Antonio

Oh, widow Dido? Ay, widow Dido.

Gonzalo

jacket [*to* **Alonso**] Is not, sir, my doublet° as fresh as the first
way day I wore it? I mean, in a sort°—

Antonio

[*to* **Sebastian**] That "sort" was well fished for.   100

Gonzalo

When I wore it at your daughter's marriage.

Alonso

You cram these words into mine ears against
appetite The stomach° of my sense. [2] Would I had never
Married my daughter there, for, coming thence,
estimation My son is lost and, in my rate,° she too,   105
Who is so far from Italy removed
I ne'er again shall see her.—O thou mine heir
Of Naples and of Milan, what strange fish
Hath made his meal on thee?

Francisco

                                                Sir, he may live.
surging waves I saw him beat the surges° under him   110
And ride upon their backs. He trod the water,
Whose enmity he flung aside, and breasted
The surge most swoll'n that met him. His bold head
'Bove the contentious waves he kept, and oared
Himself with his good arms in lusty stroke   115
To th' shore, that o'er his wave-worn basis bowed, [3]

1   *loose*

    This is the spelling of the 1623
    Folio, meaning "release," though
    it is not impossible the intended
    word is "lose."

2   *Where she at least is banished from your*
    eye, / Who hath cause to wet the grief on 't

    Where she is at least absent from
    your eye, which has reason to weep
    in sorrow

3   *Weighed between loathness and*
    obedience, at / Which end o' th' beam
    should bow

    I.e., balanced, as on a scale, between
    reluctance and obedience,
    pondering which should prevail.
    Claribel could not choose between a
    desire to obey her father and a
    loathing of the task he asked of her
    (to marry the King of Tunis).

4   *of this business' making*

    I.e., from the making of this
    marriage. Though one woman was
    wed, the shipwreck (which,
    Sebastian assumes, has resulted in
    the death of many sailors) has
    turned many women in Naples and
    Milan into widows.

As if / do not As° stooping to relieve him. I not° doubt

He came alive to land.

Alonso

No, no, he's gone.

Sebastian

Sir, you may thank yourself for this great loss,

That would not bless our Europe with your daughter, 120

But rather loose¹ her to an African,

Where she at least is banished from your eye,

Who hath cause to wet the grief on 't.²

Alonso

Prithee, peace.

Sebastian

begged You were kneeled to and importuned° otherwise

By all of us, and the fair soul herself 125

Weighed between loathness and obedience, at

Which end o' th' beam should bow.³ We have lost your
son,

I fear, forever. Milan and Naples have

More widows in them of this business' making⁴

Than we bring men to comfort them. 130

The fault's your own.

Alonso

i.e., Ferdinand So is the dear'st° o' th' loss.

Gonzalo

My lord Sebastian,

The truth you speak doth lack some gentleness

fitting time And time° to speak it in. You rub the sore

bandage When you should bring the plaster.°

Sebastian

Very well. 135

Antonio

like a surgeon And most chirurgeonly.°

1   *plantation*

    The word *plantation*, stemming (as
    Antonio's deliberately literal
    mockery recognizes) from
    agriculture, is synonymous with
    colonization in general but
    originates in particular, according to
    OED, from the ongoing attempts by
    the English to "pacify" and "civilize"
    their Irish neighbors. Gonzalo's
    visionary speech closely echoes the
    phrasing of a passage from Florio's
    English translation of Montaigne's
    essay "Of the Cannibals" (1578–1580),
    which offers an idealized vision of
    native Brazilians designed to
    highlight European corruption. The
    repetition of negative definitions—
    no kind, no name—also calls to mind
    Thomas More's influential *Utopia*
    and its ambivalent attitude toward
    colonial enterprise.

2   *docks, or mallows*

    Two kinds of weeds that serve as
    balm for nettle stings

3   *by contraries*

    Contrary to common practice

4   *Bourn, bound of land*

    Boundaries between individuals'
    properties. Gonzalo would
    eliminate private property.

5   *The latter end of his commonwealth*
    forgets the beginning.

    I.e., there's an inherent contradiction
    in wanting to be king (line 141) over a
    nation that rejects sovereign power.

Gonzalo

[*to* **Alonso**] It is foul weather in us all, good sir,
When you are cloudy.

Sebastian

                Foul weather?

Antonio

                          Very foul.

Gonzalo

Had I plantation[1] of this isle, my lord—

Antonio

[*to* **Sebastian**] He'd sow 't with nettle-seed.

Sebastian

                    Or docks, or mallows.[2]   140

Gonzalo

if I were And were° the king on 't, what would I do?

Sebastian

lack [*to* **Antonio**] 'Scape being drunk for want° of wine.

Gonzalo

I' th' commonwealth I would by contraries[3]
commerce Execute all things, for no kind of traffic°
judge Would I admit. No name of magistrate.°   145
literature; i.e., erudition Letters° should not be known. Riches, poverty,
servitude / inheritance And use of service°—none. Contract, succession,°
farm cultivation Bourn, bound of land,[4] tilth,° vineyard—none.
grain No use of metal, corn,° or wine, or oil.
No occupation: all men idle, all.   150
merely And women too, but° innocent and pure.
No sovereignty—

Sebastian

              [*to* **Antonio**] Yet he would be king on 't.

Antonio

The latter end of his commonwealth forgets the
beginning.[5]

1   *in common*

    For common use

2   *knaves*

    Base and crafty rogues

3   *Golden Age*

    **The idealized, original period of
    human history described by the
    Greek poet Hesiod (in *Works and Days*)
    and expanded upon by the Roman
    poet Ovid (in *Metamorphoses*). The
    first age of humankind was
    characterized by a supreme
    innocence and abundance and was
    completely lacking in strife,
    struggle, or greed. The Golden Age
    eventually degenerated into the
    increasingly corrupt Silver, Bronze,
    Heroic, and Iron Ages.**

4   *minister occasion*

    **Give these men occasion (for
    laughter). Gonzalo believes that
    Sebastian and Antonio would crack
    jokes in any case, so he chooses to
    give them cause for their laughter.**

5   *use to laugh*

    Make habit of laughing

Gonzalo

All things in common [1] nature should produce   155
Without sweat or endeavor. Treason, felony,
Sword, pike, knife, gun, or need of any engine
Would I not have, but nature should bring forth,
plenty Of its own kind, all foison,° all abundance,
To feed my innocent people.   160

Sebastian

[*to* **Antonio**] No marrying 'mong his subjects?

Antonio

[*to* **Sebastian**] None, man. All idle. Whores and knaves. [2]

Gonzalo

I would with such perfection govern, sir,
T' excel the Golden Age. [3]

Sebastian

God save 'Save° his Majesty!   165

Antonio

Long live Gonzalo!

Gonzalo

And—do you mark me, sir?

Alonso

nonsense Prithee, no more. Thou dost talk nothing° to me.

Gonzalo

I do well believe your Highness, and did it to minister
occasion [4] to these gentlemen, who are of such sensi-   170
sensitive ble° and nimble lungs that they always use to laugh [5]
at nothing.

Antonio

'Twas you we laughed at.

Gonzalo

Who, in this kind of merry fooling, am nothing to you;
so you may continue and laugh at nothing still.   175

1 *An it had not fallen flat-long.*

If it had not been delivered with the flat side of the sword (hence, less harmful than if with the edge).

2 *You would lift the moon out of her sphere, if she would continue in it five weeks without changing.*

I.e., you would move the very moon out of its orbit, if it stayed constant for five weeks.

3 *a-batfowling*

(1) literally, catching birds at night with the use of long poles, called *bats*, to beat the birds out of the trees; (2) figuratively, taking advantage of a simpleton (i.e., someone as dumb as a bird)

4 *I will not adventure my discretion so weakly*

I.e., I won't risk my reputation for intelligence on so weak a cause as the feeble jokes you make at my expense

5 *Would, with themselves, shut up my thoughts*

I.e., would, when I close them, shut out thoughts (as well as sights)

6 *Do not omit the heavy offer of it. / It seldom visits sorrow.*

Do not ignore the gift of sleep. It rarely comes to those in sorrow.

Antonio

What a blow was there given!

Sebastian

An it had not fallen flat-long. ¹

Gonzalo

spirit You are gentlemen of brave mettle.° You would lift the
moon out of her sphere, if she would continue in it five
weeks without changing. ²   *180*

Enter **Ariel** [*,invisible,*] *playing solemn music.*

Sebastian

We would so, and then go a-batfowling. ³

Antonio

Nay, good my lord, be not angry.

Gonzalo

No, I warrant you, I will not adventure my discretion so
sleepy weakly. ⁴ Will you laugh me asleep, for I am very heavy?°

Antonio

Go sleep, and hear us.   *185*

[*All except* **Alonso**, **Sebastian**, *and* **Antonio** *sleep.*]

Alonso

What? All so soon asleep? I wish mine eyes
Would, with themselves, shut up my thoughts. ⁵ I find
They are inclined to do so.

Sebastian

Please you, sir,
ignore Do not omit° the heavy offer of it.
It seldom visits sorrow. ⁶ When it doth,   *190*
It is a comforter.

Antonio

We two, my lord,
Will guard your person while you take your rest,

1　*art thou waking?*

　　**I.e., are you serious? Sebastian
　　expresses alarm at Antonio's
　　suggestion of treason.**

And watch your safety.

Alonso

Thank you. Wondrous heavy.

[**Alonso** *falls asleep.* **Ariel** *exits.*]

Sebastian

What a strange drowsiness possesses them!

Antonio

character   It is the quality° o' th' climate.

Sebastian

Why   195

Doth it not then our eyelids sink? I find not

Myself disposed to sleep.

Antonio

Nor I. My spirits are nimble.

They fell together all, as by consent.

They dropped as by a thunderstroke. What might,

Worthy Sebastian, oh, what might—? No more.   200

And yet methinks I see it in thy face

What thou shouldst be. Th' occasion speaks thee, and

My strong imagination sees a crown

Dropping upon thy head.

Sebastian

What, art thou waking?[1]

Antonio

Do you not hear me speak?

Sebastian

I do, and surely   205

It is a sleepy language, and thou speak'st

Out of thy sleep. What is it thou didst say?

This is a strange repose, to be asleep

With eyes wide open, standing, speaking, moving,

And yet so fast asleep.

1   *wink'st*

    I.e., you shut your eyes

2   *You / Must be so too if heed me, which to*
    do / Trebles thee o'er.

    **You must also be serious if you
follow my advice, which, if you do,
will make you three times greater
than you are now.**

3   *standing water*

    **Still water not affected by the tides;
i.e., waiting to be pushed in a
direction**

4   *To ebb / Hereditary sloth instructs me.*

    **Either (1) my natural laziness or (2) my
subordinate position as Alonso's
younger brother holds me back.**

5   *If you but knew how you the purpose*
    cherish / Whiles thus you mock it

    **If only you realized how much you
desire (to advance yourself), even
as you mock that very ambition**

6   *A matter*

    I.e., something important

7   *a birth indeed / Which throes thee much*
    to yield

    **I.e., talking about (giving birth to)
that matter is causing you much
effort and pain.**

8   *this lord of weak remembrance*

    **This lord with a bad memory (i.e.,
Gonzalo)**

Antonio

Noble Sebastian, 210
Thou let'st thy fortune sleep—die, rather; wink'st[1]
Whiles thou art waking.

Sebastian

Thou dost snore distinctly.
There's meaning in thy snores.

Antonio

customary practice I am more serious than my custom.° You
Must be so too if heed me, which to do 215
Trebles thee o'er.[2]

Sebastian

Well, I am standing water.[3]

Antonio

i.e., advance; move I'll teach you how to flow.°

Sebastian

Do so. To ebb
Hereditary sloth instructs me.[4]

Antonio

Oh,
If you but knew how you the purpose cherish
Whiles thus you mock it,[5] how in stripping it 220
clothe (ceremonially) You more invest° it! Ebbing men indeed
Most often do so near the bottom run
By their own fear or sloth.

Sebastian

Prithee, say on.
fixed look The setting° of thine eye and cheek proclaim
A matter[6] from thee, and a birth indeed 225
Which throes thee much to yield.[7]

Antonio

Thus, sir:
Although this lord of weak remembrance[8]—this,

1　*Who shall be of as little memory / When*
　he is earthed

**Who shall be just as poorly
remembered when he is buried**

2　*only / Professes to persuade*

**I.e. his only occupation is
persuasion**

3　*No hope that way is / Another way so*
　high a hope that even / Ambition cannot
　pierce a wink beyond, / But doubt
　discovery there.

**I.e., having no hope that Ferdinand
has not drowned leads to a higher
hope (of the crown), beyond which
ambition cannot aspire without
fearing discovery. The syntax is
confused, perhaps suggesting
Antonio's agitation, or perhaps it is
a deliberate effort to avoid directly
expressing his intentions.**

4　*beyond man's life*

**I.e., further than a man can travel
in a lifetime**

5　*till new-born chins / Be rough and razorable*

**I.e., Claribel will not receive any
messages from Naples before
those who are now infants are old
enough to grow beards.**

Who shall be of as little memory
When he is earthed [1]—hath here almost persuaded
(For he's a spirit of persuasion, only   230
Professes to persuade [2]) the King his son's alive,
'Tis as impossible that he's undrowned
As he that sleeps here swims.

Sebastian
                                        I have no hope
That he's undrowned.

Antonio
                                        Oh, out of that "no hope"
What great hope have you! No hope that way is   235
Another way so high a hope that even
Ambition cannot pierce a wink beyond,
But doubt discovery there. [3] Will you grant with me
That Ferdinand is drowned?

Sebastian
                                        He's gone.

Antonio
                                                    Then, tell me,
Who's the next heir of Naples?

Sebastian
                                        Claribel.   240

Antonio
She that is Queen of Tunis; she that dwells
Ten leagues beyond man's life; [4] she that from Naples
news / messenger   Can have no note,° unless the sun were post°—
The man i' th' moon's too slow—till new-born chins
i.e., coming from   Be rough and razorable; [5] she that from° whom   245
cast up on shore   We all were sea-swallowed, though some cast° again,
And by that destiny to perform an act
Whereof what's past is prologue, what to come
performance   In yours and my discharge.°

1   *cubit*

Ancient unit of length, roughly
18–22 inches

2   *I myself could make / A chough of as deep chat.*

I.e., I myself could train a jackdaw
(*chough*, a kind of chattering crow)
to speak as meaningfully as he
does.

3   *And how does your content / Tender your
own good fortune?*

I.e., do you look with pleasure on
your good fortune?

4   *conscience*

Conscience, the internal voice that
prompted ethical practice, was a key
word in the process of the
Reformation. For Protestants, the
promptings of conscience overrode
the rules of the Church and entitled
the individual to resist certain aspects
of longstanding Catholic doctrine.
Antonio's lack of conscience would
characterize him, for Calvinists in the
audience (who were by no means all
opposed to the theater, as is
sometimes assumed), as a *reprobate*,
i.e. one of the damned, with the
implication—problematized by his
dabbling in occult arts—of
Prospero's status as *elect*, i.e., one of
the few bound for Heaven.

Sebastian

What stuff is this? How say you?
'Tis true, my brother's daughter's Queen of Tunis;   250
So is she heir of Naples, 'twixt which regions
There is some space.

Antonio

A space whose every cubit[1]
Seems to cry out, "How shall that Claribel
i.e., Return / Stay Measure° us back to Naples? Keep° in Tunis
And let Sebastian wake." Say this were death   255
That now hath seized them. Why, they were no worse
those who Than now they are. There be that° can rule Naples
chatter As well as he that sleeps, lords that can prate°
As amply and unnecessarily
As this Gonzalo. I myself could make   260
i.e., if only A chough of as deep chat.[2] Oh that° you bore
The mind that I do; what a sleep were this
For your advancement! Do you understand me?

Sebastian

Methinks I do.

Antonio

And how does your content
Tender your own good fortune?[3]

Sebastian

I remember   265
overthrow You did supplant° your brother Prospero.

Antonio

True.
And look how well my garments sit upon me,
more suitably Much feater° than before. My brother's servants
comrades Were then my fellows.° Now they are my men.

Sebastian

But for your conscience?[4]   270

1   *If 'twere a kibe, / 'Twould put me to my*
    slipper.

    I.e., if my conscience were a
    chilblain (a sore on the foot), it
    would make me wear a slipper.

2   *And melt ere they molest*

    And dissolve before they bother me

3   *perpetual wink for aye*

    Closing of Gonzalo's eyes forever

4   *They'll tell the clock to any business that /*
    We say befits the hour.

    They will chime in agreement with us
    that it is the right time to do whatever
    we determine. (I.e., they will
    unquestioningly follow whatever
    course of action we suggest.)

Antonio

Ay, sir. Where lies that? If 'twere a kibe,
'Twould put me to my slipper,¹ but I feel not
This deity in my bosom. Twenty consciences

congealed That stand 'twixt me and Milan, candied° be they
And melt ere they molest!² Here lies your brother,   275
No better than the earth he lies upon,
If he were that which now he's like—that's dead—

sword Whom I, with this obedient steel,° three inches of it,
Can lay to bed forever, whiles you, doing thus,
To the perpetual wink for aye³ might put   280
This ancient morsel, this Sir Prudence, who

censure / As for Should not upbraid° our course. For° all the rest,
follow They'll take° suggestion as a cat laps milk.
They'll tell the clock to any business that
We say befits the hour.⁴

Sebastian

                    Thy case, dear friend,   285
Shall be my precedent. As thou got'st Milan,
I'll come by Naples. Draw thy sword. One stroke
Shall free thee from the tribute which thou payest,
And I the King shall love thee.

Antonio

                    Draw together,
same thing And when I rear my hand, do you the like°   290
To fall it on Gonzalo.

          [**Antonio** *and* **Sebastian** *draw their swords.*]

Sebastian

               Oh, but one word.

Enter **Ariel** [*, invisible,*] *with music and song.*

1   *them*

I.e., Gonzalo and Antonio

2   *you drawn*

Your swords drawn

Ariel

[*to* **Gonzalo**] My master through his art foresees the
    danger

That you, his friend, are in, and sends me forth—

otherwise For else° his project dies—to keep them[1] living.

                                            (*sings in* **Gonzalo**'s *ear*)

While you here do snoring lie,   295

Open-eyed conspiracy

opportunity His time° doth take.

If of life you keep a care,

Shake off slumber and beware:

Awake, awake!   300

Antonio

[*to* **Sebastian**] Then let us both be sudden.

Gonzalo

[*waking and seeing them*] Now good angels preserve the
    King.

Alonso

[*waking*] Why, how now? Ho, awake!   [*Everyone awakes.*]
    Why are you drawn?[2]

fearful Wherefore this ghastly° looking?

Gonzalo

                                        What's the matter?

Sebastian

guarding Whiles we stood here securing° your repose,   305

Even now, we heard a hollow burst of bellowing

Like bulls, or rather lions. Did 't not wake you?

It struck mine ear most terribly.

Alonso

                                    I heard nothing.

1   They exit.

    **Ariel most likely exits through a
different door than the courtiers use.**

Antonio

Oh, 'twas a din to fright a monster's ear—
To make an earthquake! Sure, it was the roar   310
Of a whole herd of lions.

Alonso

                                        Heard you this, Gonzalo?

Gonzalo

Upon mine honor, sir, I heard a humming,
And that a strange one too, which did awake me.
I shaked you, sir, and cried. As mine eyes opened,
I saw their weapons drawn. There was a noise,   315
true   That's verily.° 'Tis best we stand upon our guard
leave Or that we quit° this place. Let's draw our weapons.

Alonso

Lead off this ground, and let's make further search
For my poor son.

Gonzalo

                              Heavens keep him from these beasts,
surely For he is sure° i' th' island.

Alonso

                                        Lead away.   320

Ariel

[*aside*] Prospero, my lord, shall know what I have done.
So, King, go safely on to seek thy son.   *They exit.* [1]

1 *By inchmeal*

   Inch by inch

2 *urchin-shows*

   Goblin like apparitions; spirits
   shaped like *urchins* (hedgehogs)

3 *bear off*

   Protect against; keep off

4 *bombard*

   Leather jug that held alcohol,
   which took its name from an early
   type of cannon

Act 2, Scene 2

*Enter **Caliban** with a burden of wood.*
A noise of thunder heard.

Caliban

All the infections that the sun sucks up

marshes / i.e., Prospero From bogs, fens, flats,° on Prosper° fall and make him

By inchmeal¹ a disease! His spirits hear me,

neither And yet I needs must curse. But they'll nor° pinch,

Fright me with urchin-shows,² pitch me i' th' mire,   5

torch Nor lead me like a firebrand° in the dark

Out of my way, unless he bid 'em. But

For every trifle are they set upon me:

grimace; make faces Sometime like apes that mow° and chatter at me,

And after bite me, then like hedgehogs which   10

Lie tumbling in my barefoot way and mount

Their pricks at my footfall. Sometime am I

entwined All wound° with adders who with cloven tongues

Do hiss me into madness.

*Enter **Trinculo**.*

Lo, now, lo!

Here comes a spirit of his, and to torment me   15

For bringing wood in slowly. I'll fall flat.

notice Perchance he will not mind° me. [*lies down, covering himself*
with his cloak]

Trinculo

Here's neither bush nor shrub to bear off³ any weather

at all, and another storm brewing; I hear it sing i' th'

Yonder wind. Yond° same black cloud, yond huge one, looks   20

like a foul bombard⁴ that would shed his liquor.

1   *Poor-John*

Dried fish, usually salted hake, a
staple food for those living in poverty

2   *painted*

I.e., painted on a sign to attract
onlookers

3   *not a holiday fool there but would give a
piece of silver*

I.e., there isn't a gullible person
there who wouldn't give a piece of
silver to see it

4   *make a man*

(1) provide his master with a fortune
in revenue; (2) pass for a real man

5   *dead Indian*

Exhibitions featuring Native
Americans were popular
entertainments in Elizabethan
London.

6   *o' my troth*

I.e., by my faith

7   *gaberdine*

A cloak made of coarse material

8   *dregs*

Literally, the sediment at the bottom
of a liquor bottle; a continuation of
the *bombard* simile in 2.2.21

9   *swabber*

Sailor who cleans the deck of a ship

10 *tang*

Sting (i.e., she has a sharp tongue)

If it should thunder as it did before, I know not where
to hide my head. Yond same cloud cannot choose but
fall by pailfuls. [*sees* **Caliban**] What have we here? A
man or a fish? Dead or alive? A fish. He smells like a   25
fish. A very ancient and fish-like smell, a kind of not-of-
the-newest Poor-John. [1] A strange fish! Were I in
England now, as once I was, and had but this fish
painted, [2] not a holiday fool there but would give a
piece of silver. [3] There would this monster make a man. [4]   30
Any strange beast there makes a man. When they will
small coin not give a doit° to relieve a lame beggar, they will lay out
ten to see a dead Indian. [5] Legged like a man and his fins
like arms! Warm, o' my troth! [6] I do now let loose my opinion, hold it no longer: this is no fish, but an islander   35
perished that hath lately suffered° by a thunderbolt. [*thunder*]
Alas, the storm is come again! My best way is to creep
under his gaberdine. [7] There is no other shelter here-
about. Misery acquaints a man with strange bedfellows. I
take cover will here shroud° till the dregs [8] of the storm be past.   40
[*crawls under* **Caliban**'*s gaberdine*]

Enter **Stephano**, *singing*.

Stephano

    I shall no more to sea, to sea,
    Here shall I die ashore—
contemptible This is a very scurvy° tune to sing at a man's funeral.
Well, here's my comfort. (*drinks, sings*)
    The master, the swabber, [9] the boatswain and I,   45
    The gunner and his mate
    Loved Mall, Meg, and Marian and Margery,
    But none of us cared for Kate.
    For she had a tongue with a tang, [10]

1   *a tailor might scratch her where'er she*
    did itch
    The implication here is that even a
    tailor (a profession that was
    frequently associated with a lack of
    virility) could satisfy Kate's sexual
    desire.

2   *What's the matter?*
    I.e., what's going on?

3   *Do you put tricks upon 's*
    I.e., are you trying to play tricks
    on me

4   *went on four legs*
    Stephano misquotes the proverb
    "As good a man as ever went on
    two legs." Since Caliban and
    Trinculo are hiding under the
    gaberdine cloak, Stephano can
    only see their legs and assumes all
    four belong to a single creature.

5   *ague*
    A fever that often causes shivering

6   *talk after the wisest*
    Speak wisely

7   *go near to*
    Do much to

8   *I will not take too much for him.*
    I.e., no amount of money will be
    too high for him. Stephano, like
    Trinculo at 2.2.27–30, imagines
    displaying Caliban as a curiosity to
    paying spectators.

9   *He shall pay for him that hath him*
    He will pay heavily who wants to
    buy him (from me)

Would cry to a sailor, "Go hang!"   50
She loved not the savor of tar nor of pitch,
Yet a tailor might scratch her where'er she did itch. [1]
Then to sea, boys, and let her go hang!
This is a scurvy tune too. But here's my comfort. (*drinks*)

Caliban

Do not torment me! Oh!   55

Stephano

What's the matter? [2] Have we devils here? Do you put
India   tricks upon 's [3] with savages and men of Ind?° Ha! I have
not 'scaped drowning to be afeard now of your four legs,
for it hath been said, "As proper a man as ever went on
four legs [4] cannot make him give ground," and it shall   60
be said so again while Stephano breathes at th' nostrils.

Caliban

The spirit torments me! Oh!

Stephano

This is some monster of the isle with four legs who
hath got, as I take it, an ague. [5] Where the devil should
he learn our language? I will give him some relief, if it   65
cure   be but for that. If I can recover° him and keep him tame
and get to Naples with him, he's a present for any
cow's   emperor that ever trod on neat's° leather.

Caliban

[*to* **Trinculo**] Do not torment me, prithee. I'll bring my
wood home faster.   70

Stephano

He's in his fit now and does not talk after the wisest. [6]
He shall taste of my bottle. If he have never drunk wine
afore, it will go near to [7] remove his fit. If I can recover
him and keep him tame, I will not take too much for
him. [8] He shall pay for him that hath him, [9] and that   75
soundly.

1   *thy trembling*

    Trinculo is shaking with fear.

2   *Come on your ways.*

    Let's get going.

3   *Here is that which will give language to*
    you, cat.

    Following a proverbial expression,
    "liquor that would make a cat speak"

4   *delicate*

    Exquisitely made; ingenious

5   *If all the wine in my bottle will recover*
    him

    I.e., even if it takes all of the wine
    that I have left

6   *long spoon*

    According to the proverb, "He
    must have a long spoon that eats
    with the devil."

Caliban

[*to* **Trinculo**] Thou dost me yet but little hurt. Thou wilt anon, I know it by thy trembling. [1] Now Prosper works upon thee.

Stephano

[*trying to give* **Caliban** *drink*] Come on your ways. [2] Open 80
your mouth. Here is that which will give language to
get rid of   you, cat. [3] Open your mouth. This will shake° your
shaking, I can tell you, and that soundly. You cannot
jaws   tell who's your friend. Open your chaps° again.

Trinculo

I should know that voice. It should be—but he is 85
drowned, and these are devils. Oh, defend me!

Stephano

Four legs and two voices—a most delicate [4] monster.
His forward voice now is to speak well of his friend. His
backward voice is to utter foul speeches and to detract.
If all the wine in my bottle will recover him, [5] I will help 90
i.e., Enough   his ague. Come. [**Caliban** *drinks.*] Amen!° I will pour
some in thy other mouth.

Trinculo

Stephano!

Stephano

Doth thy other mouth call me? Mercy, mercy! This is a devil
and no monster. I will leave him. I have no long spoon. [6] 95

Trinculo

Stephano! If thou be'st Stephano, touch me and speak
to me. For I am Trinculo. Be not afeard—thy good
friend Trinculo.

Stephano

If thou be'st Trinculo, come forth. I'll pull thee by the
lesser legs. If any be Trinculo's legs, these are they. 100
[*pulls* **Trinculo** *out from under the cloak*]

1   *mooncalf*

Monster; deformed being. It was
believed that birth defects were
caused by the moon.

2   *an if*

If

3   *butt of sack*

Cask of sweet white wine

4   *kiss the book*

I.e., take a drink. Stephano combines
the proverbial expression "kiss the
cup" with the practice of kissing the
Bible when swearing an oath.

5   *a goose*

Trinculo's neck is stretched out as he
drinks from the bottle; Stephano
also implies that Trinculo is
unsteady on his feet.

truly   Thou art very° Trinculo indeed! How cam'st thou to be
dung / excrete   the siege° of this mooncalf?¹ Can he vent° Trinculos?

Trinculo

I took him to be killed with a thunder-stroke. But art
thou not drowned, Stephano? I hope now thou art not
drowned. Is the storm overblown? I hid me under the   105
dead mooncalf's gaberdine for fear of the storm. And art
thou living, Stephano? O Stephano, two Neapolitans

escaped   'scaped!°   [*hugs* **Stephano**]

Stephano

Prithee, do not turn me about; my stomach is
not constant.   110

Caliban

spirits   [*aside*] These be fine things, an if² they be not sprites.°
glorious   That's a brave° god, and bears celestial liquor. I will
kneel to him.

Stephano

[*to* **Trinculo**] How didst thou 'scape? How cam'st thou
hither? Swear by this bottle how thou cam'st hither. I   115
escaped upon a butt of sack³ which the sailors heaved
o'erboard, by this bottle, which I made of the bark of a
tree with mine own hands since I was cast ashore.

Caliban

[*to* **Stephano**] I'll swear upon that bottle to be thy true
subject, for the liquor is not earthly.   120

Stephano

[*to* **Trinculo**] Here. Swear then how thou escaped'st.

Trinculo

Swum ashore, man, like a duck. I can swim like a duck,
I'll be sworn.

Stephano

Here, kiss the book.⁴ [**Trinculo** *drinks.*] Though thou
canst swim like a duck, thou art made like a goose.⁵   125

1 *when time was*
   Once upon a time

2 *thy dog and thy bush*
   According to legend, the man in
   the moon was banished there with
   his dog for stealing a bundle of
   sticks (i.e., a thorn *bush*).

3 *By this good light*
   I.e., in the sunlight

4 *monster*
   The word *monster* is repeated
   frequently in the play, and not only
   whenever Europeans address or
   discuss Caliban: to the
   Neapolitans, everything seems
   monstrous, from the *strange shapes
   bringing in a banquet* to the invisible
   voices of the island. The repetition
   in the case of Caliban is designed
   to install a sense in the audience of
   his lack of humanity even as his
   words seem to establish his human
   sensitivity. Caliban is treated by
   Prospero as a monster because of
   his apparent ingratitude, by
   Miranda because he tried to rape
   her, and by Stephano and Trinculo
   because of their home-grown
   preconceptions about "monstrous
   births" and fairground displays.
   Mark Thornton Burnett
   interestingly argues that by the
   end of the play, when he pleads
   with the audience for release,
   Prospero himself has, partly due to
   his questionable powers and partly

to his acknowledgment of a certain
kinship with Caliban, become
monstrous.

5 *in good sooth*
   In truth (a common oath)

Trinculo

O Stephano, hast any more of this?

Stephano

cask / wine cellar The whole butt,° man. My cellar° is in a rock by th'
seaside where my wine is hid.—How now, mooncalf!
How does thine ague?

Caliban

Hast thou not dropped from Heaven?   130

Stephano

Out o' th' moon, I do assure thee. I was the man i' th'
moon when time was. ¹

Caliban

I have seen thee in her, and I do adore thee. My
mistress showed me thee and thy dog and thy bush. ²

Stephano

Come; swear to that; kiss the book. I will furnish it   135
anon with new contents. Swear. [**Caliban** *drinks.*]

Trinculo

gullible By this good light, ³ this is a very shallow° monster! ⁴ I
afeard of him? A very weak monster! The man i' th'
drunk moon? A most poor, credulous monster!—Well drawn,°
monster, in good sooth! ⁵   140

Caliban

[*to* **Stephano**] I'll show thee every fertile inch o' th'
island, and I will kiss thy foot. I prithee, be my god.

Trinculo

treacherous By this light, a most perfidious° and drunken monster!
When 's god's asleep, he'll rob his bottle.

Caliban

[*to* **Stephano**] I'll kiss thy foot. I'll swear myself thy   145
subject.

Stephano

Come on then: down and swear.

1   *kiss*

Stephano offers his hand (or
perhaps his foot) to Caliban to *kiss*
as a sign of respect.

2   *make a wonder of*

Wonder at; be amazed by

3   *crabs*

Either crabapples or, possibly,
crustaceans living in rockpools.

4   *scamels*

Of uncertain meaning. It is
commonly emended to "seameal"
or "sea mew," which are variants of
seagull, though it may be an
unrecorded variant of a word
meaning "shellfish."

5   *bear my bottle*

Probably directed to Caliban

Trinculo

I shall laugh myself to death at this puppy-headed
monster. A most scurvy monster! I could find in my
heart to beat him—   150

Stephano

[*to* **Caliban**] Come, kiss. [1]

Trinculo

his cups (i.e., drunk) —but that the poor monster's in drink.° An abominable
monster!

Caliban

I'll show thee the best springs. I'll pluck thee berries.
I'll fish for thee and get thee wood enough.   155
A plague upon the tyrant that I serve!
I'll bear him no more sticks, but follow thee,
Thou wondrous man.

Trinculo

A most ridiculous monster, to make a wonder of[2] a
poor drunkard!   160

Caliban

[*to* **Stephano**] I prithee, let me bring thee where crabs[3]
    grow.
edible tubers And I with my long nails will dig thee pignuts,°
Show thee a jay's nest, and instruct thee how
a small monkey To snare the nimble marmoset.° I'll bring thee
hazelnuts To clust'ring filberts,° and sometimes I'll get thee   165
Young scamels[4] from the rock. Wilt thou go with me?

Stephano

I prithee now, lead the way without any more talking.
—Trinculo, the King and all our company else being
take possession drowned, we will inherit° here.—Here, bear my bottle.[5]
it —Fellow Trinculo, we'll fill him° by and by again.   170

Caliban

Farewell master! Farewell, farewell.

1   *Get a new man.*

    **Caliban addresses Prospero, his
    old master.**

Trinculo

A howling monster, a drunken monster.

Caliban

to trap (*sings drunkenly*) No more dams I'll make for° fish,

firewood Nor fetch in firing,° at requiring,

trenchers; wooden plates Nor scrape trenchering,° nor wash dish. 175

'Ban, 'Ban, Ca-caliban

Has a new master. Get a new man. [1]

holiday Freedom, high-day,° high-day, freedom, freedom,

high-day, freedom!

Stephano

O brave monster! Lead the way. *They exit.* 180

1   *their labor / Delight in them sets off*

   **The pleasure dervied from them
   compensates for the effort**

2   *Had never like executor*

   **I.e., never had such a (worthy and
   handsome) person performing it**

3   *I forget*

   I.e., I forget to work

4   *Most busil'est when I do it*

   **I.e., most busily refreshing when I
   am working my hardest**

5   *'Twill weep*

   **It will weep (by oozing resin as it
   burns)**

Act 3, Scene 1

*Enter **Ferdinand** bearing a log.*

Ferdinand

activities   There be some sports° are painful, and their labor
menial tasks   Delight in them sets off. [1] Some kinds of baseness°
           Are nobly undergone, and most poor matters
lowly   Point to rich ends. This my mean° task
except that   Would be as heavy to me as odious, but°   5
enlivens   The mistress which I serve quickens° what's dead
           And makes my labors pleasures. Oh, she is
irritable   Ten times more gentle than her father's crabbed,°
           And he's composed of harshness. I must remove
           Some thousands of these logs and pile them up,   10
harsh   Upon a sore° injunction. My sweet mistress
           Weeps when she sees me work and says such baseness
           Had never like executor. [2] I forget, [3]
           But these sweet thoughts do even refresh my labors,
           Most busil'est when I do it. [4]

*Enter **Miranda** and **Prospero**[, who is unseen].*

Miranda

                        Alas, now pray you,   15
wish   Work not so hard. I would° the lightning had
commanded   Burnt up those logs that you are enjoined° to pile!
i.e., this wood   Pray, set it down and rest you. When this° burns,
           'Twill weep [5] for having wearied you. My father
           Is hard at study. Pray now, rest yourself.   20
harmless   He's safe° for these three hours.

Ferdinand

                       O most dear mistress,
complete   The sun will set before I shall discharge°

1   *worm*

Prospero's affectionate term for Miranda emphasizes her human frailty.

2   *visitation*

Visit. A play on the idea that love is a kind of plague *visited* on lovers

3   *broke your hest*

Disobeyed your order

4   *Admired Miranda*

The Latin word *miranda* means "admirable" or "wonderful," so Ferdinand is making an obvious pun on his new girlfriend's name. He is also stating overtly the controlling emotion of the play— and of the other Shakespearean "late plays"—namely, wonder. Wonder operates in several ways in the play: on a practical level, it is the product of costume and staging and operates as a control on the audience, keeping them guessing by manipulating their generic expectations; on an ideological level, Prospero's magic works by inspiring fear and awe in the others and in instilling into them a sense of unreality and disorientation that allows him to fulfill his dynastic plan.

What I must strive to do.
Miranda

                              If you'll sit down,
I'll bear your logs the while. Pray, give me that;
I'll carry it to the pile.
Ferdinand

                              No, precious creature;   25
I had rather crack my sinews, break my back,
Than you should such dishonor undergo
While I sit lazy by.
Miranda

suit   It would become° me
As well as it does you, and I should do it
With much more ease, for my good will is to it   30
And yours it is against.
Prospero

                              [*aside*] Poor worm,¹ thou art infected!
This visitation² shows it.
Miranda

weary   You look wearily.°
Ferdinand
No, noble mistress; 'tis fresh morning with me
nearby When you are by° at night. I do beseech you—
Chiefly that I might set it in my prayers—   35
What is your name?
Miranda

                              Miranda.—O my father,
I have broke your hest³ to say so!
Ferdinand

                              Admired Miranda!⁴
Indeed the top of admiration, worth
most valuable What's dearest° to th' world! Full many a lady

1   *so full soul*

    With such a perfect soul

2   *put it to the foil*

    Challenged it, defeated it (a term used in fencing)

3   *created / Of every creature's best*

    Made up of the best attributes of every living thing

4   *How features are abroad / I am skilless of*

    What people look like in other places, I do not know

5   *Nor can imagination form a shape / Besides yourself to like of*

    Nor can I imagine that I would like any appearance other than yours

6   *I would not so!*

    I wish it were not the case!

7   *wooden slavery*

    Referring to his task of moving the wooden logs

8   *to suffer / The flesh fly blow my mouth*

    Allow the *flesh fly* (which lays its eggs in dead flesh) to contaminate my mouth with its eggs

I have eyed with best regard, and many a time   40
Th' harmony of their tongues hath into bondage
attentive / various Brought my too diligent° ear. For several° virtues
Have I liked several women. Never any
With so full soul, [1] but some defect in her
owned Did quarrel with the noblest grace she owed°   45
And put it to the foil. [2] But you, O you,
So perfect and so peerless, are created
Of every creature's best! [3]
Miranda
                                        I do not know
One of my sex, no woman's face remember,
mirror Save, from my glass,° mine own. Nor have I seen   50
More that I may call men than you, good friend,
And my dear father. How features are abroad
chastity I am skilless of, [4] but, by my modesty,°
dowry The jewel in my dower,° I would not wish
Any companion in the world but you,   55
Nor can imagination form a shape
Besides yourself to like of. [5] But I prattle
Somewhat Something° too wildly, and my father's precepts
I therein do forget.
Ferdinand
rank   I am in my condition°
A prince, Miranda; I do think a king   60
—I would not so! [6]—and would no more endure
This wooden slavery [7] than to suffer
The flesh fly blow my mouth. [8] Hear my soul speak:
The very instant that I saw you did
My heart fly to your service, there resides   65
To make me slave to it, and for your sake
Am I this patient log-man.

1   *If hollowly, invert / What best is boded*
     me to mischief!

     If I speak untruly, let the best
     things that are fated to happen to
     me turn to ill fortune!

2   *to want*

     For lack of

3   *all the more it seeks to hide itself / The*
     bigger bulk it shows

     Miranda suggests that her love for
     Ferdinand is like a secret pregnancy,
     which becomes increasingly
     apparent despite (or perhaps
     because of) her attempts to hide it.

4   *maid*

     Maidservant; also, chaste woman

Miranda

Do you love me?

Ferdinand

O Heaven, O Earth, bear witness to this sound

outcome And crown what I profess with kind event°

If I speak true! If hollowly, invert   70

What best is boded me to mischief! [1] I,

whatever Beyond all limit of what° else i' th' world,

Do love, prize, honor you.

Miranda

I am a fool

To weep at what I am glad of.

Prospero

[*aside*] Fair encounter

Of two most rare affections! Heavens rain grace   75

On that which breeds between 'em!

Ferdinand

Why   Wherefore° weep you?

Miranda

At mine unworthiness that dare not offer

What I desire to give, and much less take

What I shall die to want. [2] But this is trifling,

And all the more it seeks to hide itself   80

The bigger bulk it shows. [3] Hence, bashful cunning,

And prompt me, plain and holy innocence!

I am your wife, if you will marry me;

companion If not, I'll die your maid. [4] To be your fellow°

You may deny me, but I'll be your servant   85

Whether you will or no.

Ferdinand

My mistress, dearest,

And I thus humble ever.

1   *as willing / As bondage e'er of freedom*

   As desirous (of marriage) as a slave
   is of freedom

2   *A thousand thousand!*

   I.e., a million farewells!

3   *Who are surprised withal*

   Who are astonished by it

4   *appertaining*

   Relating to (their union)

Miranda

My husband, then?

Ferdinand

                                    Ay, with a heart as willing
As bondage e'er of freedom. [1] Here's my hand.

Miranda

And mine, with my heart in 't. And now farewell   90
Till half an hour hence.

Ferdinand

                              A thousand thousand! [2]

                                                  They exit [separately].

Prospero

So glad of this as they I cannot be,
Who are surprised withal, [3] but my rejoicing
At nothing can be more. I'll to my book,
For yet ere supper-time must I perform   95
Much business appertaining. [4]   *He exits.*

1   *bear up and board 'em*

A naval command to sail toward
and attack the enemy. Here it
means "drink up."

2   *set*

Placed. (Trinculo takes Stephano's
language literally.)

3   *five and thirty leagues*

Roughly 100 miles (a league is a
measure of distance of about three
miles)

4   *off and on*

Toward and away from the shore

5   *By this light*

A mild oath

6   *He's no standard.*

I.e., he can't stand upright
(punning on *standard* in line 15)

7   *run*

Run away (from an enemy)

8   *lie*

Lie down; also, "tell lies"

Act 3, Scene 2

Enter **Caliban**, **Stephano**, *and* **Trinculo**.

Stephano

cask   Tell not me. When the butt° is out, we will drink water,
not a drop before. Therefore bear up and board 'em.[1]
—Servant-monster, drink to me.

Trinculo

absurdity   "Servant-monster"? The folly° of this island. They say
there's but five upon this isle. We are three of them. If   5
addle-brained   th' other two be brained° like us, the state totters.

Stephano

Drink, servant-monster, when I bid thee. Thy eyes are
fixed (by drunkenness)   almost set° in thy head.

Trinculo

splendid   Where should they be set[2] else? He were a brave° monster
indeed if they were set in his tail.   10

Stephano

sweet wine   My man-monster hath drowned his tongue in sack.° For
my part, the sea cannot drown me. I swam, ere I could
recover the shore, five and thirty leagues[3] off and on.[4] By
this light,[5] thou shalt be my lieutenant, monster, or
standard-bearer   my standard.°   15

Trinculo

please   Your lieutenant, if you list.° He's no standard.[6]

Stephano

We'll not run,[7] Monsieur Monster.

Trinculo

walk   Nor go° neither. But you'll lie[8] like dogs and yet say
nothing neither.

Stephano

Mooncalf, speak once in thy life, if thou be'st a good   20
mooncalf.

1 *I am in case to jostle a constable.*

   I am prepared (because valiant through drink) to push a policeman.

2 *natural*

   I.e., an idiot (a pun on the fact that monsters are un*natural*)

3 *keep a good tongue in your head*

   A proverbial expression meaning "watch what you say"

4 *the next tree*

   I.e., the next tree will be the gallows upon which you are hanged

5 *Marry*

   Indeed; to be sure (a mild oath meaning, "by [the Virgin] Mary")

Caliban

How does thy Honor? Let me lick thy shoe.

[*indicating* **Trinculo**] I'll not serve him. He's not valiant.

Trinculo

Thou liest, most ignorant monster. I am in case to jostle a

i.e., debauched   constable. [1] Why, thou deboshed° fish, thou, was there   25

ever man a coward that hath drunk so much sack as I

today? Wilt thou tell a monstrous lie, being but half a

fish and half a monster?

Caliban

Lo, how he mocks me! Wilt thou let him, my lord?

Trinculo

"Lord," quoth he! That a monster should be such   30

a natural! [2]

Caliban

Lo, lo, again! Bite him to death, I prithee.

Stephano

Trinculo, keep a good tongue in your head. [3] If you

prove a mutineer, the next tree. [4] The poor monster's

my subject, and he shall not suffer indignity.   35

Caliban

I thank my noble lord. Wilt thou be pleased to hearken

request   once again to the suit° I made to thee?

Stephano

Marry, [5] will I. Kneel and repeat it. I will stand, and so

shall Trinculo.

Enter **Ariel**, *invisible.*

Caliban

[*kneeling*] As I told thee before, I am subject to a tyrant, a   40

sorcerer, that by his cunning hath cheated me of the

island.

1   *knock a nail into his head*

     In Judges 4:21, Jael murders Sisera
     in this fashion.

2   *What a pied ninny's this!* [to **Trinculo**]
     Thou scurvy patch!

     Trinculo, whose name derives
     from the Italian for "drinking
     heavily," is described in the Folio's
     List of Roles as a *jester*, that is, a
     professional clown retained as a
     source of amusement by a royal
     household. Such official jesters
     were given license to be offensive
     and wore motley, that is, a multi-
     colored costume, which is perhaps
     the source of an alternative name
     for a fool, *patch* (*OED* notes that the
     household fool of Cardinal Wolsey
     in the reign of Henry VIII was
     named Patch). There are several
     such jesters in Shakespeare's plays,
     notably Feste in *Twelfth Night* and
     the Fool in *King Lear*, and the
     question of whether or not they are
     actually *ninnies* (i.e., genuinely
     simple) is repeatedly raised
     because of the quick-wittedness
     required to perform the task of
     fooling successfully.

Ariel

[*as* **Trinculo**] Thou liest.

Caliban

[*to* **Trinculo**] Thou liest, thou jesting monkey, thou! I
would my valiant master would destroy thee. I do not lie.   45

Stephano

Trinculo, if you trouble him any more in 's tale, by this
uproot   hand, I will supplant° some of your teeth.

Trinculo

Why, I said nothing.

Stephano

Mum, then, and no more. [*to* **Caliban**] Proceed.

Caliban

I say by sorcery he got this isle;   50
From me he got it. If thy greatness will
Revenge it on him—for I know thou dar'st,
i.e., Caliban himself   But this thing° dare not—

Stephano

That's most certain.

Caliban

Thou shalt be lord of it, and I'll serve thee.   55

Stephano

accomplished   How now shall this be compassed?° Canst thou bring
individual (i.e., Prospero)   me to the party?°

Caliban

Yea, yea, my lord. I'll yield him thee asleep
Where thou mayst knock a nail into his head. [1]

Ariel

[*as* **Trinculo**] Thou liest. Thou canst not.   60

Caliban

What a pied ninny's this! [*to* **Trinculo**] Thou scurvy patch! [2]
[*to* **Stephano**] I do beseech thy greatness, give him blows
And take his bottle from him. When that's gone

1   *quick freshes*

    Flowing streams of fresh water

2   *make a stock-fish of thee*

    **I.e., beat you. Dried fish (i.e., *stock-*
    ***fish*) were beaten to tenderize them
    before cooking.**

3   *give me the lie*

    Say that I am lying

4   *There thou mayst brain him*

    Then you may break his skull

He shall drink nought but brine, for i'll not show him
Where the quick freshes¹ are.   65

Stephano

Trinculo, run into no further danger. Interrupt the
monster one word further, and, by this hand, I'll turn
my mercy out o' doors and make a stock-fish of thee. ²

Trinculo

Why? What did I? I did nothing. I'll go farther off.

Stephano

Didst thou not say he lied?   70

Ariel

[*as* **Trinculo**] Thou liest.

Stephano

[*to* **Trinculo**] Do I so? Take thou that. [*beats* **Trinculo**] As
you like this, give me the lie³ another time.

Trinculo

I did not give the lie. Out o' your wits and hearing too?
A pox° o' your bottle! This° can sack and drinking do. A   75
murrain° on your monster, and the devil take your fingers!

plague / This is what
plague

Caliban

Ha, ha, ha!

Stephano

Now, forward with your tale. [*to* **Trinculo**] Prithee, stand
farther off.

Caliban

Beat him enough. After a little time,   80
I'll beat him too.

Stephano

[*to* **Stephano**] Stand farther. [*to* **Caliban**] Come, proceed.

Caliban

Why, as I told thee, 'tis a custom with him
I' th' afternoon to sleep. There thou mayst brain him, ⁴
Having first seized his books, or with a log   85

1 *paunch*

   Stab in the stomach

2 *brave utensils*

   **Splendid goods (a reference to
   either Prospero's household
   possessions or his tools for magic,
   either of which would seem
   impressive to Caliban)**

3 *deck withal*

   Decorate (the house) with (them)

Batter his skull, or paunch [1] him with a stake,

windpipe Or cut his weasand° with thy knife. Remember

First to possess his books, for without them

fool He's but a sot,° as I am, nor hath not

One spirit to command. They all do hate him   90

deeply As rootedly° as I. Burn but his books.

He has brave utensils, [2] for so he calls them,

Which when he has a house he'll deck withal. [3]

And that most deeply to consider is

The beauty of his daughter. He himself   95

thing without equal Calls her a nonpareil.° I never saw a woman

Except /mother But° only Sycorax my dam° and she,

But she as far surpasseth Sycorax

As great'st does least.

Stephano

splendid   Is it so brave° a lass?

Caliban

suit Ay, lord. She will become° thy bed, I warrant,   100

And bring thee forth brave brood.

Stephano

Monster, I will kill this man. His daughter and I will be

i.e., God save king and queen—save° our graces!—and Trinculo and

governors thyself shall be viceroys.°—Dost thou like the plot,

Trinculo?   105

Trinculo

Excellent.

Stephano

Give me thy hand. I am sorry I beat thee. But while thou

liv'st, keep a good tongue in thy head.

Caliban

Within this half hour will he be asleep.

Wilt thou destroy him then?

1   *but whilere*

    A little while ago

2   tabor and pipe

    A *tabor* is a round drum that hangs at the musician's side; the *pipe* is designed to be played with one hand while the other beats the tabor.

3   *the picture of Nobody*

    I.e., an invisible person. *Nobody* is a character in the 1606 play *Nobody and Some-body*, and was depicted on the play's title page as a man with a head, arms, and legs but no trunk.

4   *He that dies pays all debts.*

    A proverbial expression; when one *dies*, one is freed from the obligation of paying off *debts*.

Stephano

Ay, on mine honor.   110

Ariel

[*aside*] This will I tell my master.

Caliban

Thou mak'st me merry. I am full of pleasure.

merry / sing / song   Let us be jocund.° Will you troll° the catch°

You taught me but whilere?[1]

Stephano

whatever is reasonable   At thy request, monster; I will do reason,° any reason.   115

—Come on, Trinculo, let us sing.

[*sings*] Flout 'em and scout 'em,

And scout 'em and flout 'em.

Thought is free.

Caliban

That's not the tune.   120

Ariel *plays the tune on a tabor and pipe.*[2]

Stephano

What is this same?

Trinculo

This is the tune of our catch, played by the picture of

Nobody.[3]

Stephano

[*calls to the music*] If thou be'st a man, show thyself in thy

true form / wish   likeness.° If thou be'st a devil, take 't as thou list.°   125

Trinculo

Oh, forgive me my sins!

Stephano

He that dies pays all debts.[4]—I defy thee!—Mercy

upon us!

Caliban

Art thou afeard?

1 *music for nothing*

Perhaps a topical reference to the fact that England's King James I spent large amounts of money on musicians and court entertainments

2 *lays it on*

I.e., plays his music with vigor

Stephano

No, monster, not I.   130

Caliban

Be not afeard. The isle is full of noises,

melodies   Sounds and sweet airs° that give delight and hurt not.

twanging   Sometimes a thousand twangling° instruments

Will hum about mine ears, and sometime voices

at that moment   That, if I then° had waked after long sleep,   135

Will make me sleep again; and then, in dreaming,

it seemed to me   The clouds methought° would open and show riches

Ready to drop upon me, that when I waked

I cried to dream again.

Stephano

This will prove a brave kingdom to me, where I shall   140

have my music for nothing. ¹

Caliban

When Prospero is destroyed.

Stephano

That shall be by and by. I remember the story.

[**Ariel** *exits, playing.*]

Trinculo

The sound is going away. Let's follow it and after do our

work.   145

Stephano

Lead, monster; we'll follow. I would I could see this

taborer. He lays it on. ²

Trinculo

[*to* **Caliban**] Wilt come? I'll follow Stephano.   *They exit.*

1   *By 'r lakin*

    **By our ladykin; a milder form of the
    oath "by our Lady"**

2   *forthrights and meanders*

    Straight paths and winding paths

3   *for one repulse*

    On account of one stumbling block

Act 3, Scene 3

Enter **Alonso**, **Sebastian**, **Antonio**, **Gonzalo**, **Adrian**,
Francisco, *and others.*

Gonzalo
[*to* **Alonso**] By 'r lakin, [1] I can go no further, sir.
My old bones ache. Here's a maze trod indeed
Through forthrights and meanders. [2] By your patience,
I needs must rest me.

Alonso
                Old lord, I cannot blame thee,
seized Who am myself attached° with weariness   5
To th' dulling of my spirits. Sit down and rest.
Even here I will put off my hope and keep it
as No longer for° my flatterer. He is drowned
Whom thus we stray to find, and the sea mocks
useless Our frustrate° search on land. Well, let him go.   10

Antonio
[*aside to* **Sebastian**] I am right glad that he's so out of
    hope.
Do not, for one repulse, [3] forego the purpose
That you resolved t' effect.

Sebastian
               [*aside to* **Antonio**] The next advantage
thoroughly Will we take throughly.°

Antonio
              [*aside to* **Sebastian**] Let it be tonight,
For now they are oppressed with travail. They   15
Will not, nor cannot, use such vigilance
As when they are fresh.

1   on the top

Many Renaissance theaters
featured a balcony above the stage
where the musicians sat (see Fig. 1
on page 252); Prospero appears on
this balcony.

2   *living drollery*

Puppet shows with live actors,
instead of wooden puppets

3   *phoenix'*

The *phoenix* is a mythical Arabian
bird—only one living at any
moment—that lives for five
hundred years and then reincarnates
itself by bursting into flames and
rising again from its own ashes.

4   *what does else want credit*

Anything else that lacks credibility

5   *Travelers ne'er did lie*

A reference to the proverb, "A
traveler may lie with authority."

Sebastian

> [*aside to* **Antonio**] I say tonight. No more.

> *Solemn and strange music. [Enter] **Prospero** on the top,* [1]
> *invisible.*

Alonso

What harmony is this? My good friends, hark!

Gonzalo

Marvelous sweet music!

> *Enter several strange shapes, bringing in a banquet and*
> *dance about it with gentle actions of salutations, and inviting*
> *the King etc. to eat, they depart.*

Alonso

guardian angels   Give us kind keepers,° heavens! What were these?   20

Sebastian

A living drollery. [2] Now I will believe

That there are unicorns, that in Arabia

There is one tree, the phoenix' [3] throne, one phoenix

At this hour reigning there.

Antonio

                                    I'll believe both;

And what does else want credit, [4] come to me,   25

And I'll be sworn 'tis true. Travelers ne'er did lie, [5]

Though fools at home condemn 'em.

Gonzalo

                                    If in Naples

I should report this now, would they believe me?

If I should say I saw such islanders—

certainly   For certes° these are people of the island   30

1   *want the use of tongue*

    I.e., lack a spoken language

2   *Praise in departing.*

    Save your praise until the end.

3   *mountaineers / Dewlapped like bulls*

    Mountain-dwellers with folds of
    skin under their necks, like bulls

4   *Each putter-out of five for one will bring
    us / Good warrant of*

    A reference to the form of
    insurance that venturers took out
    before going on a mercantile
    voyage, making overt the close
    connection between capital
    ventures, insurance, and
    gambling. The traveler left a sum of
    money with a broker before
    starting out; if the traveler
    returned with proof that he had
    reached his destination, then the
    money would be paid back
    fivefold; if not, the broker kept the
    original sum. Even at what seems
    like excellent odds, the broker had
    a clear advantage, such ventures
    being so hazardous. The *putter-out*
    here could be either the venturer
    or the broker. *Good warrant* is
    either's report of the success or
    failure of the venture.

Who, though they are of monstrous shape, yet note
Their manners are more gentle, kind, than of
Our human generation you shall find
Many—nay, almost any.

Prospero

                              [*aside*] Honest lord,
Thou hast said well, for some of you there present   35
Are worse than devils.

Alonso

marvel at   I cannot too much muse°
Such shapes, such gesture, and such sound expressing,
Although they want the use of tongue, [1] a kind
silent   Of excellent dumb° discourse.

Prospero

                              [*aside*] Praise in departing. [2]

Francisco

They vanished strangely.

Sebastian

                              No matter, since   40
food / appetites   They have left their viands° behind, for we have stomachs.°
Will 't please you taste of what is here?

Alonso

                                             Not I.

Gonzalo

Faith, sir, you need not fear. When we were boys,
Who would believe that there were mountaineers
Dewlapped like bulls, [3] whose throats had hanging at 'em   45
Wattles; Pouches   Wallets° of flesh, or that there were such men
Whose heads stood in their breasts, which now we find
Each putter-out of five for one will bring us
testimony   Good warrant° of. [4]

1 like

In the shape of

2 harpy

A mythological creature with the head and torso of a woman and the body and wings of a bird, with talons for hands. In the *Aeneid*, Aeneas and his men encounter the harpies, who destroy the feast that they have prepared.

3 quaint device

Quaint meant something quite different to Shakespeare's contemporaries than it does to us: it implies a blend of imagination, skill and elegance, along with a certain strangeness or novelty. A *device* is a mechanism of some sort—or at least a hidden person—to make the banquet vanish in a split second. This stage direction reminds us that complex and effective staging has been part of the play's life right from the beginning and that the audience's wonder at such stage-trickery is an integral part of the play's intended effect. The rather awestruck phrasing here may well be that of the King's Company's scribe Ralph Crane, who was probably responsible for the manuscript used as the basis for the First Folio text.

4 *never-surfeited*

Never filled; never satisfied

5 *such-like valor*

I.e., courage that stems from madness

6 *The elements / Of whom your swords are tempered*

I.e., the materials out of which your swords are fashioned

7 *still-closing*

Always coming back together

8 *massy*

Heavy. Ariel uses his magic to make the swords too heavy to be lifted.

9 *my business to you*

I.e., my purpose in coming to you

Alonso

begin to eat   I will stand to and feed,°

Although my last. No matter, since I feel   50

The best is past. Brother, my lord the Duke,

Stand to and do as we.

Thunder and lightning. Enter **Ariel** *like*[1] *a harpy,*[2] *claps his*
wings upon the table, and, with a quaint device,[3] *the*
banquet vanishes.

Ariel

[*to* **Alonso**, **Antonio**, *and* **Sebastian**] You are three
    men of sin, whom destiny,

as its   That hath to° instrument this lower world

And what is in 't, the never-surfeited[4] sea   55

Hath caused to belch up you, and on this island

Where man doth not inhabit, you 'mongst men

Being most unfit to live. I have made you mad,

And even with such-like valor[5] men hang and drown

own   Their proper° selves. [*Some of the courtiers draw their swords.*]

    You fools! I and my fellows   60

Are ministers of fate. The elements

Of whom your swords are tempered[6] may as well

Wound the loud winds, or with bemocked-at stabs

Kill the still-closing[7] waters, as diminish

tiny feather   One dowl° that's in my plume. My fellow ministers   65

similarly   Are like° invulnerable. If you could hurt,

Your swords are now too massy[8] for your strengths

And will not be uplifted. But remember—

For that's my business to you[9]—that you three

From Milan did supplant good Prospero,   70

revenged   Exposed unto the sea, which hath requit° it,

Him and his innocent child. For which foul deed

1   *and do pronounce by me*

   **And (the *powers*), using me as their
   agent, sentence you to**

2   *Ling'ring perdition*

   Slow destruction; living Hell

3   *whose wraths*

   I.e., the anger of the *powers*

4   *is nothing*

   There is no alternative

5   mows

   Grimaces

6   *devouring*

   **I.e., in removing the food from the
   table in such a way that it looked as
   if it was being eaten by a harpy.**

7   *So, with good life / And observation
   strange, my meaner ministers / Their
   several kinds have done.*

   **In the same convincing manner
   and with remarkable attentiveness
   my lesser spirits have performed
   their various roles.**

The powers°—delaying, not forgetting—have
deities

Incensed the seas and shores, yea, all the creatures,

Against your peace. Thee of thy son, Alonso,   75

They have bereft, and do pronounce by me [1]

Ling'ring perdition, [2] worse than any death

Can be at once, shall step by step attend

You and your ways, whose wraths [3] to guard you from—

Which here, in this most desolate isle, else° falls   80
otherwise

Upon your heads—is nothing [4] but hearts' sorrow

And a clear life ensuing.

> [**Ariel**] *vanishes in thunder. Then, to soft music, enter the*
> *Shapes again and dance, with mocks and mows, [5] and*
> *carrying out the table.*

Prospero

Bravely the figure of this harpy hast thou

Performed, my Ariel. A grace it had, devouring. [6]

Of my instruction hast thou nothing bated°   85
omitted

In what thou hadst to say. So,° with good life
In the same way

And observation strange, my meaner ministers

Their several kinds have done. [7] My high charms work,

And these, mine enemies, are all knit° up
tangled

In their distractions. They now are in my power;   90

And in these fits I leave them, while I visit

Young Ferdinand, whom they suppose is drowned,

And his and mine loved darling.   [*He exits.*]

Gonzalo

[*to* **Alonso**] I' th' name of something holy, sir, why
stand you

In this strange stare?

Alonso

Oh, it is monstrous, monstrous!   95

1   *It did bass my trespass*

    (1) it told of my sin in a deep (i.e.,
    bass) voice; (2) it provided
    accompaniment to the treble
    singing of the winds; (3) it intensified
    the baseness of my deeds

2   *plummet*

    A weight used to measure the
    depth of water

3   *But one fiend at a time, / I'll fight their
    legions o'er.*

    As long as they came one at a time, I
    would fight all the legions of
    demons.

4   *second*

    Assistant (a dueling term)

5   *given to work a great time after*

    That does not work immediately
    but is deadly at some later time

Methought the billows spoke and told me of it;
The winds did sing it to me, and the thunder,
That deep and dreadful organ pipe, pronounced
The name of Prosper. It did bass my trespass. [1]
For this reason Therefore° my son i' th' ooze is bedded, and   100
I'll seek him deeper than e'er plummet [2] sounded
And with him there lie mudded.   *He exits.*
Sebastian

                                        But one fiend at a time,
I'll fight their legions o'er. [3]
Antonio

                                        I'll be thy second. [4]
                          [**Sebastian** *and* **Antonio**] *exit.*
Gonzalo

despairing; reckless All three of them are desperate.° Their great guilt,
Like poison given to work a great time after, [5]   105
Now 'gins to bite the spirits. I do beseech you
That are of suppler joints, follow them swiftly
madness And hinder them from what this ecstasy°
May now provoke them to.
Adrian

                                        Follow, I pray you. *They exit.*

1   *a third of mine own life*

Editors have disagreed about Prospero's meaning here. The *third* might simply be generic (at 5.1.311, he refers to *every third thought*, simply meaning something he is thinking about a great deal); equally, it might be that bringing up Miranda, who is 15, has taken a third of his life (making Prospero at 45 much younger than he is generally portrayed on stage); or else he has two other thirds in mind, which editors have variously suggested might be his dead wife, his magic, or his dukedom. The early editor Lewis Theobald argued that "third" was a compositor's misreading for "thread," which is not impossible.

2   *gift*

The Folio reading is "guest," which Rowe, in 1709 first emended to *gift*, a choice editors have mostly echoed since. (Crane, the scribe, characteristically spelled *gift* as "guift" and, with the Jacobean long "s," the two words would be almost identical to the eye.) The emendation underlines what is already clear in the speech—that Miranda as a young marriageable virgin within a patriarchal culture is deployed as a means of creating a bond of kinship between two men of different families to the benefit of both.

3   *Against an oracle*

I.e., even if divine prophecy said otherwise

4   *break her virgin-knot*

Virgin-knot here means "hymen," perhaps alluding to the Latin expression "unloose the girdle," implying the availability of a virgin, though the idea of breaking a knot implies more violence than this, especially in view of Ariel's erstwhile imprisonment within a *knotty pine*. Prospero's threat to Ferdinand here seems extraordinarily harsh, but underlines not only Prospero's discomfort with Miranda's sexuality but also the characteristics required for a successful exchange relationship within patriarchy: without the maintenance of her virginity prior to the legal rite of marriage and thus without the guarantee of legitimacy for her children, Miranda would cease to have value as an object of exchange between families; the grander the families involved, the grimmer the fallout if the rules are ignored.

5   *Hymen's lamps*

Hymen, the Greek god of marriage, was said to carry a wedding torch that would burn clear for a favorable marriage and smoky for an ill-fated union.

Act 4, Scene 1

Enter **Prospero**, **Ferdinand**, *and* **Miranda**.

Prospero

harshly   [*to* **Ferdinand**] If I have too austerely° punished you,
Your compensation makes amends, for I
Have given you here a third of mine own life [1]—
whom   Or that for which I live—who° once again
offer   I tender° to thy hand. All thy vexations   5
Were but my trials of thy love, and thou
wonderfully   Hast strangely° stood the test. Here, afore heaven,
I ratify this my rich gift. [2] O Ferdinand,
Do not smile at me that I boast of her,
For thou shalt find she will outstrip all praise   10
limp   And make it halt° behind her.

Ferdinand

                         I do believe it
Against an oracle. [3]

Prospero

Then, as my gift and thine own acquisition
Worthily purchased, take my daughter. But
If thou dost break her virgin-knot [4] before   15
All sanctimonious ceremonies may
With full and holy rite be ministered,
shower   No sweet aspersion° shall the heavens let fall
To make this contract grow, but barren hate,
Sour-eyed disdain, and discord shall bestrew   20
loathsome   The union of your bed with weeds so loathly°
That you shall hate it both. Therefore take heed,
As Hymen's lamps [5] shall light you.

Ferdinand

                         As I hope
children   For quiet days, fair issue,° and long life,

1   *the strong'st suggestion / Our worser*
    genius can

    I.e., the strongest temptation our
    evil spirit can make

2   *to take away / The edge of that day's*
    celebration, / When I shall think or
    Phoebus' steeds are foundered / Or night
    kept chained below

    To satisfy the desire of our wedding
    day, when it shall seem to me
    either that the sun will never set, or
    that night will never come. The
    Roman god *Phoebus* was said to pull
    the sun across the sky in his horse-
    drawn chariot; *foundered* = lame.

3   *What*

    An exclamation that Prospero uses
    to call Ariel

4   *meaner fellows*

    Lesser spirits

5   *vanity of mine art*

    I.e., a trifling display of my art.
    Working within Renaissance
    conventions of self-deprecation,
    Prospero plays down what is in fact
    an elaborate entertainment for the
    marriage of Miranda and Ferdinand
    based on the court masque.
    Masques were principally formal,
    complex dances, following a clear
    structure and designed to glorify
    either the monarch or a couple at
    their wedding—or both if the
    wedding took place in the presence
    of the monarch. Inigo Jones and
    Shakespeare's friend and rival Ben
    Jonson were, at the time *The Tempest*
    was written, creating the Jacobean
    court masque as a form, producing a
    major entertainment every year for
    king, courtiers, and diplomats from
    foreign countries. The masque here
    is consciously formal and classical
    (Ceres, Juno, and Iris were Greek and
    Roman goddesses) and follows the
    pattern established by Jonson and
    Jones—except that the antimasque,
    a brief intrusion by the forces of
    chaos, which usually begins the
    Jacobean masque before being
    driven out by the clarity and order of
    the dance, is taking place
    simultaneously in the form of the
    rebellion of Caliban, Trinculo, and
    Stephano, the belated recollection
    of which by Prospero shatters his
    concentration and makes the vision
    of the masque *heavily vanish*.

6   *with a twink*

    I.e., in the wink of the eye

With such love as 'tis now, the murkiest den,   25
The most opportune place, the strong'st suggestion
Our worser genius can,[1] shall never melt
Mine honor into lust to take away
The edge of that day's celebration,

either When I shall think or° Phoebus' steeds are foundered   30
Or night kept chained below.[2]

Prospero

                          Fairly spoke.

Sit then and talk with her; she is thine own.
—What,[3] Ariel! My industrious servant, Ariel!

Enter **Ariel**.

Ariel

What would my potent master? Here I am.

Prospero

Thou and thy meaner fellows[4] your last service   35
Did worthily perform, and I must use you

i.e., lesser spirits In such another trick. Go bring the rabble,°
O'er whom I give thee power, here to this place.
Incite them to quick motion, for I must
Bestow upon the eyes of this young couple   40
Some vanity of mine art.[5] It is my promise,
And they expect it from me.

Ariel

Immediately   Presently?°

Prospero

Ay, with a twink.[6]

Ariel

Before you can say "Come" and "Go,"
And breathe twice and cry "So, so!"   45
Each one, tripping on his toe,

1   *true*

    I.e., true to your word

2   *Do not give dalliance / Too much the rein.*

    Do not give your amorous thoughts too much freedom.

3   *good night*

    I.e., farewell to; forget

4   *ardor of my liver*

    The *liver* was considered the seat of passion.

5   *Bring a corollary / Rather than want a spirit.*

    I.e., bring extra spirits, rather than risk having too few.

6   **Iris**

    Iris, messenger of the gods, begins the masque. As goddess of the rainbow she would likely appear in colorful attire (hence *many-colored messenger* in 4.1.76).

7   *Ceres*

    Goddess of earth, agriculture, and harvest. Known to the Greeks as *Demeter*.

8   *vetches*

    Plants grown for fodder

9   *meads thatched with stover them to keep*

    I.e., meadows covered with hay to feed the sheep

10 *Thy banks with pionèd and twillèd brims*

    A much debated phrase; it may mean (1) your banks, which have been dug with trenches and reinforced with woven sticks to prevent erosion; (2) your banks, which natural erosion has marked with trenches and braidlike patterns; or possibly (3) an error for your banks, which have peonies and lillies at the edges.

11 *thy hest betrims*

    At thy bidding trims (with flowers)

i.e., grimaces Will be here with mop and mow.°
Do you love me, master? No?
Prospero
Dearly, my delicate Ariel. Do not approach
Till thou dost hear me call.
Ariel

understand   Well; I conceive.°   *He exits.*   50
Prospero
[*to* **Ferdinand**] Look thou be true.¹ Do not give dalliance
Too much the rein.² The strongest oaths are straw
To th' fire i' th' blood. Be more abstemious,
Or else good night³ your vow!
Ferdinand

                              I warrant you, sir,
The white cold virgin snow upon my heart   55
Abates the ardor of my liver.⁴
Prospero

                           Well.
—Now come, my Ariel! Bring a corollary
quickly Rather than want a spirit.⁵ Appear, and pertly!°

                                        Soft music.

[*to* **Miranda** *and* **Ferdinand**] No tongue, all eyes! Be
   silent.

Enter **Iris**.⁶

Iris
fields Ceres,⁷ most bounteous lady, thy rich leas°   60
Of wheat, rye, barley, vetches,⁸ oats, and peas;
grassy Thy turfy° mountains where live nibbling sheep,
And flat meads thatched with stover them to keep;⁹
Thy banks with pionèd and twillèd brims,¹⁰
rainy Which spongy° April at thy hest betrims¹¹   65

1   *broomgroves*

   Cluster of yellow-flowered shrubs

2   *Being lass-lorn*

   I.e., having lost his love

3   *leave these*

   **I.e., leave the various places
   described**

4   *Her peacocks fly amain.*

   **Her peacocks (which draw her
   chariot) fly quickly. The** *peacock*
   **was a sacred bird to Juno, queen
   of the gods and wife of Jupiter.**

5   *Rich scarf*

   I.e., Iris (as a rainbow)

6   *Venus or her son*

   **Venus was the goddess of love;
   her son was Cupid.**

7   *they did plot / The means that dusky Dis
   my daughter got*

   **Venus and Cupid made Pluto, god
   of the underworld, fall in love
   with Ceres' daughter Prosperine,
   whom he then kidnapped and
   married.**

chaste	To make cold° nymphs chaste crowns; and thy
	broom-groves,¹
rejected	Whose shadow the dismissèd° bachelor loves,
i.e., pruned	Being lass-lorn;² thy poll-clipped° vineyard
beach	And thy sea-marge,° sterile and rocky-hard,
	Where thou thyself dost air—the queen o' th' sky, *70*
rainbow	Whose watery arch° and messenger am I,
	Bids thee leave these,³ and with her sovereign grace,

                    Juno [*partially*] *descends.*

	Here on this grass plot, in this very place,
	To come and sport. Her peacocks fly amain.⁴
greet	Approach, rich Ceres, her to entertain.° *75*

       Enter **Ceres**.

Ceres

	Hail, many-colored messenger, that ne'er
	Dost disobey the wife of Jupiter,
	Who, with thy saffron wings, upon my flowers
	Diffusest honey-drops, refreshing showers;
	And with each end of thy blue bow dost crown *80*
shrub-covered / pasture	My bosky° acres and my unshrubbed down,°
	Rich scarf⁵ to my proud earth. Why hath thy Queen
	Summoned me hither to this short-grassed green?

Iris

	A contract of true love to celebrate,
bestow	And some donation freely to estate° *85*
	On the blessed lovers.

Ceres

rainbow	Tell me, heavenly bow,°
as far as	If Venus or her son,⁶ as° thou dost know,
	Do now attend the Queen? Since they did plot
	The means that dusky Dis my daughter got,⁷

1   *Paphos*

Venus's earthly home, a city on
Cyprus

2   *Dove-drawn*

Venus traveled in a chariot pulled
by doves.

3   *no bed-right shall be paid / Till Hymen's
torch be lighted*

I.e., the union will not be
consummated until after the
marriage ceremony has taken place

4   *Mars's hot minion is returned again.*

I.e., lusty Venus has gone home to
Paphos. Venus was the lover (or
minion, or "darling") of *Mars*, the
god of war.

5   *right out*

Outright (i.e., be a human child
instead of a god)

i.e., Cupid's / scandalous   Her and her blind boy's° scandaled° company   90
                              I have forsworn.

Iris
                                         Of her society
                              Be not afraid. I met her deity
                              Cutting the clouds towards Paphos,¹ and her son
                              Dove-drawn² with her. Here thought they to have done
spell   Some wanton charm° upon this man and maid,   95
                              Whose vows are that no bed-right shall be paid
                              Till Hymen's torch be lighted³—but in vain.
                              Mars's hot minion is returned again.⁴
hot-headed   Her waspish-headed° son has broke his arrows,
                              Swears he will shoot no more but play with sparrows   100
                              And be a boy right out.⁵

Ceres
                                              Highest Queen of state,
bearing   Great Juno, comes; I know her by her gait.°

                                              [**Juno** completes her descent.]

Juno
                              How does my bounteous sister? Go with me
couple   To bless this twain,° that they may prosperous be
                              And honored in their issue.   *They sing.* 105

Juno
                              [*sings*] Honor, riches, marriage-blessing,
                              Long continuance and increasing,
                              Hourly joys be still upon you.
                              Juno sings her blessings on you.

Ceres
abundance   [*sings*] Earth's increase, foison° plenty,   110
granaries   Barns and garners° never empty,
                              Vines with clust'ring bunches growing,
                              Plants with goodly burden bowing.

1 *Spring come to you at the farthest / In the very end of harvest.*

I.e., may spring come directly after autumn; may there be no winter (and thus no want)

2 *wise*

This is the most famous editorial problem in the text of *The Tempest*, a good instance of new approaches to literary interpretation influencing the work not just of critics but also of editors. In 1709 the editor Nicholas Rowe emended the Folio's "wise" to "wife" in the assumption that Ferdinand would be likely to be praising Miranda and that the scribe or compositor could easily have misread "f" as a Jacobean long "s." This was accepted for a time, but by the 19th century most editors had reverted to the Folio reading, partly because of the rhyming couplet *wise* forms with *paradise* (since the Jacobean pronunciation would probably not have differentiated voiced and unvoiced "s" quite as much as we do now). A feminist scholar, Jeanne Addison Roberts, returned to the issue in 1978, finding a copy of the Folio which suggested that early in the print run the crossbar on the "f" had broken off, making it look like a long "s" and in the process sidelining Miranda even further in a play already dominated by men.

More recently, however, both Peter Blayney and Gary Taylor have demonstrated that Roberts was probably wrong, arguing that the apparent trace of a broken crossbar that she had found is in fact an inkblot; nonetheless (and to make matters even more complex), Taylor has argued that, whether or not the compositor set an "s," Shakespeare may well have originally written *wife*. In a way, the point is that whatever choice a given editor makes, this crux underlines the mutual impact of textual editing and literary criticism.

3 *windring*

Possibly a combination of *wandering* and *winding*, but the only known example of the word

4 *sedged crowns*

Garlands of reeds

5 *crisp channels*

Rippling waters

Spring come to you at the farthest

In the very end of harvest. [1]   _115_

Scarcity and want shall shun you.

Ceres' blessing so is on you.

Ferdinand

This is a most majestic vision and

delightfully Harmonious charmingly.° May I be bold

To think these spirits?

Prospero

                                        Spirits, which by mine art   _120_

dwelling places I have from their confines° called to enact

My present fancies.

Ferdinand

                                Let me live here ever.

So rare a wondered father and a wise [2]

Makes this place Paradise.

          Juno _and_ **Ceres** _whisper and send_ **Iris** _on employment._

Prospero

                                Sweet now, silence!

Juno and Ceres whisper seriously.   _125_

There's something else to do. Hush and be mute,

Or else our spell is marred.

Iris

water nymphs You nymphs, called naiads,° of the windring [3] brooks,

With your sedged crowns [4] and ever-harmless looks,

Leave your crisp channels [5] and on this green land   _130_

Answer your summons. Juno does command.

Come, temperate nymphs, and help to celebrate

A contract of true love. Be not too late.

                    Enter certain **Nymphs**.

harvesters You sunburned sicklemen,° of August weary,

1   *encounter everyone / In country footing*

    I.e., each of you join in rustic
    dancing

2   *heavily*

    Sorrowfully

3   *movèd sort*

    Disturbed manner

4   *baseless fabric of this vision*

    The immateriality of this illusion

5   *the great globe*

    I.e., the world; also a likely allusion
    to the Globe Theatre, where most
    of Shakespeare's plays were
    performed after it was built in
    1599.

6   *all which it inherit*

    I.e., all who inhabit (the *globe*)

Come hither from the furrow and be merry. 135
Make holiday, your rye-straw hats put on,
And these fresh nymphs encounter everyone
In country footing. [1]

> *Enter certain* **Reapers**, *properly habited. They join with*
> *the* **Nymphs** *in a graceful dance, towards the end whereof*
> **Prospero** *starts suddenly and speaks.*

Prospero

[*aside*] I had forgot that foul conspiracy
Of the beast Caliban and his confederates 140
Against my life. The minute of their plot

Depart   Is almost come. [*to the spirits*] Well done! Avoid;° no more!

> *To a strange, hollow, and confused noise, they heavily* [2] *vanish.*

Ferdinand

[*to* **Miranda**] This is strange. Your father's in some
passion

agitates   That works° him strongly.

Miranda

                 Never till this day

troubled   Saw I him touched with anger so distempered.° 145

Prospero

[*to* **Ferdinand**] You do look, my son, in a movèd sort, [3]
As if you were dismayed. Be cheerful, sir.

entertainment   Our revels° now are ended. These our actors,

previously explained to   As I foretold° you, were all spirits and
Are melted into air, into thin air. 150
And, like the baseless fabric of this vision, [4]
The cloud-capped towers, the gorgeous palaces,
The solemn temples, the great globe [5] itself—
Yea, all which it inherit [6]—shall dissolve
And, like this insubstantial pageant faded, 155

1   *rounded with*

**Surrounded by; or possibly
"completed with"**

2   *with a thought*

As quickly as thought

3   *When I presented Ceres*

**Often interpreted as an indication
that Ariel acted the part of Ceres in
the masque, though it might only
mean that Ariel served as the stage
manager of the masque.**

4   *unbacked*

Never-ridden (i.e., wild; unbroken)

mist	Leave not a rack° behind. We are such stuff
of	As dreams are made on,° and our little life
	Is rounded with [1] a sleep. Sir, I am vexed.
	Bear with my weakness. My old brain is troubled.
	Be not disturbed with my infirmity. 160
	If you be pleased, retire into my cell
rest	And there repose.° A turn or two I'll walk,
agitated	To still my beating° mind.

Ferdinand, Miranda

We wish your peace. *They exit.*

Prospero

Come with a thought. [2] I thank thee, Ariel. Come.

Enter **Ariel**.

Ariel

adhere	Thy thoughts I cleave° to. What's thy pleasure? 165

Prospero

Spirit, we must prepare to meet with Caliban.

Ariel

Ay, my commander. When I presented Ceres, [3]
I thought to have told thee of it, but I feared
Lest I might anger thee.

Prospero

rogues	Say again, where didst thou leave these varlets?° 170

Ariel

	I told you, sir, they were red-hot with drinking,
beat	So full of valor that they smote° the air
	For breathing in their faces, beat the ground
maneuvering	For kissing of their feet—yet always bending°
small drum	Towards their project. Then I beat my tabor,° 175
	At which, like unbacked [4] colts, they pricked their ears,

1   *filthy-mantled*

    Scum-covered

2   *that the foul lake / O'erstunk their feet*

    I.e., so that the lake was even more
    foul smelling than their feet

3   *trumpery*

    Worthless, showy garments

4   *nature / Nurture*

    In the Renaissance, as now, the
    relative effects of birth and
    education in the development of
    moral character were a topic of
    popular debate. Prospero argues
    that for Caliban, as the child of the
    devil, education (or *Nurture*) cannot
    overcome his inherently evil *nature*.

5   glistering

    Sparkling; brilliant

6   *line*

    Most likely a reference to the *linden*
    or *lime* tree, though in the theater
    often a clothesline

Raised | Advanced° their eyelids, lifted up their noses
As if | As° they smelt music. So I charmed their ears
mooing | That, calflike, they my lowing° followed through
spiny shrubs | Toothed briers, sharp furzes,° pricking gorse, and thorns   180
 | Which entered their frail shins. At last I left them
 | I' th' filthy-mantled[1] pool beyond your cell,
 | There dancing up to th' chins, that the foul lake
 | O'erstunk their feet.[2]

Prospero

(term of endearment) | This was well done, my bird.°
 | Thy shape invisible retain thou still.   185
 | The trumpery[3] in my house, go bring it hither
bait | For stale° to catch these thieves.

Ariel

I go, I go.   *He exits.*

Prospero

A devil, a born devil, on whose nature
Nurture[4] can never stick, on whom my pains,
Humanely taken, all, all lost, quite lost.   190
And, as with age his body uglier grows,
rots / torment | So his mind cankers.° I will plague° them all,
Even to roaring.

*Enter **Ariel**, loaden with glistering[5] apparel, etc.*

Come; hang them on this line.[6]

*Enter **Caliban**, **Stephano**, and **Trinculo**, all wet.*

Caliban

Pray you, tread softly that the blind mole may
Not hear a foot fall. We now are near his cell.   195

1   *played the jack with us*

    I.e., played a mean trick on us

2   *hoodwink this mischance*

    I.e., make you forget this mishap

3   *fetch off*

    Rescue; retrieve

4   *o'er ears*

    Over my ears (i.e., drowned)

Stephano

Monster, your fairy, which you say is a harmless fairy,
has done little better than played the jack with us. [1]

Trinculo

Monster, I do smell all horse piss, at which my nose is
in great indignation.

Stephano

So is mine.—Do you hear, monster? If I should take a   200
displeasure against you, look you—

Trinculo

ruined Thou wert but a lost° monster.

Caliban

Good my lord, give me thy favor still.
Be patient, for the prize I'll bring thee to
Shall hoodwink this mischance. [2] Therefore speak softly.   205
All's hushed as midnight yet.

Trinculo

Ay, but to lose our bottles in the pool—

Stephano

There is not only disgrace and dishonor in that,
monster, but an infinite loss.

Trinculo

That's more to me than my wetting, yet this is your   210
harmless fairy, monster.

Stephano

I will fetch off [3] my bottle, though I be o'er ears [4] for my
labor.

Caliban

Prithee, my King, be quiet. See'st thou here,
This is the mouth o' th' cell. No noise, and enter.   215
Do that good mischief which may make this island
Thine own forever, and I, thy Caliban,
ever For aye° thy foot-licker.

1   *O King Stephano! O peer! O worthy*
    Stephano, look what a wardrobe here is
    for thee!

    **A reference to a popular ballad called
    "King Stephen was a worthy peer"**

2   *frippery*

    Second hand clothing shop

3   *dropsy*

    **A disease in which watery fluid
    accumulates in the tissues of the body**

4   *luggage*

    **I.e., cumbersome junk (which
    must be *lugged* around)**

5   *Mistress Line*

    **Stephano addresses the linden or *line*
    tree on which the clothing is hung.**

6   *Now is the jerkin under the line.*

    **The jacket is no longer on the
    linden tree, but rather underneath
    it; Stephano may also be
    suggesting that they are currently
    located *under the line* of the equator,
    where it was thought that tropical
    diseases could cause baldness.**

7   *Do, do. We steal by line and level, an't like*

    **I.e., yes we steal by the rules, if it
    please. *By line and level* is a
    proverbial expression meaning
    "with precision."**

8   *pass of pate*

    Witty joke; clever wordplay

Stephano

Give me thy hand. I do begin to have bloody thoughts.

Trinculo

O King Stephano! O peer! O worthy Stephano, look   220
what a wardrobe here is for thee! [1]

Caliban

Let it alone, thou fool. It is but trash.

Trinculo

Oh, ho, monster! We know what belongs to a frippery. [2]
[*puts on a gown*] O King Stephano!

Stephano

Put off that gown, Trinculo. By this hand, I'll have that   225
gown.

Trinculo

Thy Grace shall have it.

Caliban

The dropsy [3] drown this fool! What do you mean
To dote thus on such luggage? [4] Let 't alone
And do the murder first. If he awake,   230
From toe to crown he'll fill our skins with pinches,
Make us strange stuff.

Stephano

Be you quiet, monster.—Mistress Line, [5] is not this
leather jacket my jerkin?° Now is the jerkin under the line. [6] Now,
jerkin, you are like to lose your hair and prove a   235
bald jerkin.

Trinculo

Do, do. We steal by line and level, an 't like [7] your Grace.

Stephano

I thank thee for that jest. Here's a garment for 't.
Wit shall not go unrewarded while I am king of this
country. "Steal by line and level" is an excellent pass of 240
pate. [8] There's another garment for 't.

1 *lime*

   Birdlime (sticky substance used to catch birds); Trinculo urges Caliban to have sticky fingers and steal the garments

2 *barnacles*

   Either barnacles or barnacle geese (which were thought to hatch from barnacles)

3 *lay to*

   Put to use

4 divers

   Several

5 *Mountain . . . Silver . . . Fury . . . Tyrant*

   Names of the dogs that the spirits imitate

6 *charge my goblins that they grind their joints*

   Order the spirits to torment them

Trinculo

Monster, come; put some lime[1] upon your fingers and
away with the rest.

Caliban

of   I will have none on° 't. We shall lose our time

And all be turned to barnacles,[2] or to apes   245

vilely   With foreheads villainous° low.

Stephano

Monster, lay to[3] your fingers. Help to bear this away

cask   where my hogshead° of wine is, or I'll turn you out of

my kingdom. Go to; carry this.

Trinculo

And this.   250

Stephano

Ay, and this.

*A noise of hunters heard. Enter divers[4] spirits in shape of
dogs and hounds, hunting them about, **Prospero** and
Ariel setting them on.*

Prospero

Hey, Mountain, hey!

Ariel

Silver! There it goes, Silver!

Prospero

Fury, Fury! There, Tyrant,[5] there. Hark, hark!

     [*Spirits drive out **Caliban**, **Stephano**, and **Trinculo**.*]

Go; charge my goblins that they grind their joints[6]

With dry convulsions, shorten up their sinews   255

bruised   With agèd cramps, and more pinch-spotted° make them

leopard / lynx   Than pard° or cat-o-mountain.°

Ariel

                 Hark, they roar!

1   *Lies*

Elizabethan usage sometimes
permitted a singular verb with a
plural subject, especially if it
functioned as a collective noun.

Prospero

steadily   Let them be hunted soundly.° At this hour
Lies¹ at my mercy all mine enemies.
Shortly shall all my labors end, and thou   *260*
little while   Shalt have the air at freedom. For a little,°
Follow and do me service.   *They exit.*

1   *Now does my project gather to a head.*

**I.e., now my plan reaches its
culmination. Here, Prospero draws
on the language of alchemy, the
medieval chemical practice that
sought, among other goals, to
transmute base metals into gold; a
project that *gathered to a head* was an
alchemical experiment brought to
a boiling point.**

2   *time / Goes upright with his carriage*

**Time moves easily and quickly (its
burden being light since the work
is almost done)**

3   *How's the day?*

What is the time?

4   *gave in charge*

Ordered

5   *weather-fends*

Defends from bad weather

6   *abide all three distracted*

**I.e., Alonso, Sebastian, and
Antonio continue to be perplexed
and mentally troubled**

7   *winter's drops / From eaves of reeds*

**Cold rain dripping from thatched
roofs**

Act 5, Scene 1

Enter **Prospero** *in his magic robes, and* **Ariel**.

Prospero

Now does my project gather to a head. [1]

fail   My charms crack° not, my spirits obey, and time

Goes upright with his carriage. [2] How's the day? [3]

Ariel

Approaching   On° the sixth hour, at which time, my lord,

You said our work should cease.

Prospero

                    I did say so   5

When first I raised the tempest. Say, my spirit,

his   How fares the King and 's° followers?

Ariel

                      Confined together

In the same fashion as you gave in charge, [4]

Just as you left them, all prisoners, sir,

linden   In the line° grove which weather-fends [5] your cell.   10

i.e., release of them   They cannot budge till your release.° The King,

His brother, and yours, abide all three distracted, [6]

And the remainder mourning over them,

Brimful of sorrow and dismay. But chiefly

Him that you termed, sir, "the good old lord Gonzalo."   15

His tears run down his beard like winter's drops

works on   From eaves of reeds. [7] Your charm so strongly works° 'em

feelings   That, if you now beheld them, your affections°

Would become tender.

Prospero

                Dost thou think so, spirit?

Ariel

Mine would, sir, were I human.

1 *shall not myself, / One of their kind, that relish all as sharply, / Passion as they, be kindlier moved than thou art*

   I.e., shall I, human as they are, who experience emotions as acutely as they do, not be moved more by their suffering than you (who are a spirit)?

2 *with their high wrongs I am struck to th' quick*

   I am wounded deeply by their grievous acts

3 *my nobler reason 'gainst my fury / Do I take part*

   I.e., I choose the noble path of reason rather than give in to my rage

4 **Prospero**

   Prospero's conjuring of the spirits (lines 33–50) closely follows the conjuring done by Medea in Book 7 of Ovid's *Metamorphoses*.

5 *ye that on the sands with printless foot*

   Because they are immaterial, the spirits Prospero conjures will leave no footprints.

6 *ebbing Neptune*

   I.e., receding waves. *Neptune* is the Roman god of the sea.

7 *demi-puppets*

   Possibly a reference to the spirits' small stature, or to Prospero's ability to manipulate their actions

8 *green sour ringlets make, / Whereof the ewe not bites*

   Make rings of sour grass that the sheep will not eat. Known as *fairy rings*, these circles are often found at the base of mushrooms and were commonly attributed to dancing fairies.

9 *midnight mushrooms*

   Mushrooms that materialize overnight

10 *solemn curfew*

   I.e., the evening bell; the tolling of the bell would symbolize to the spirits that they were free to roam until sunrise.

11 *Weak masters*

   I.e., inferior in comparison to Prospero, but, as sprites, still powerful

12 *bedimmed / The noontide sun*

   Obscured the noon sun; i.e., caused an eclipse

13 *rifted Jove's stout oak / With his own bolt*

   I.e., split Jove's sacred oak with his own thunderbolt; *Jove*, king of the Roman gods, was known for hurling thunderbolts and for holding the oak tree sacred.

Prospero

And mine shall.   20

hint   Hast thou, which art but air, a touch,° a feeling

Of their afflictions, and shall not myself,

One of their kind, that relish all as sharply,

Feel passion   Passion° as they, be kindlier moved than thou art?[1]

Though with their high wrongs I am struck to th' quick,[2]   25

Yet with my nobler reason 'gainst my fury

more exceptional   Do I take part.[3] The rarer° action is

In virtue than in vengeance. They being penitent,

tendency   The sole drift° of my purpose doth extend

Not a frown further. Go; release them, Ariel.   30

My charms I'll break, their senses I'll restore,

And they shall be themselves.

Ariel

I'll fetch them, sir.

He exits.

Prospero[4]

[*tracing a circle on the ground*]Ye elves of hills, brooks, standing lakes, and groves,

And ye that on the sands with printless foot[5]

i.e., fly from   Do chase the ebbing Neptune[6] and do fly° him   35

When he comes back; you demi-puppets[7] that

By moonshine do the green sour ringlets make,

Whereof the ewe not bites;[8] and you whose pastime

who   Is to make midnight mushrooms,[9] that° rejoice

To hear the solemn curfew;[10] by whose aid,   40

Weak masters[11] though ye be, I have bedimmed

The noontide sun,[12] called forth the mutinous winds,

i.e., sky   And 'twixt the green sea and the azured vault°

Set roaring war—to th' dread rattling thunder

i.e., lightning   Have I given fire° and rifted Jove's stout oak   45

mountain peak   With his own bolt;[13] the strong-based promontory°

1 *graves at my command / Have waked their sleepers*

Such powers were considered grimly portentous (e.g., *Hamlet's* "A little ere the mightiest Julius fell, / The graves stood tenantless and the sheeted dead / Did squeak and gibber in the Roman streets"). It seems clear that the audience, attending church regularly and highly versed in the Bible, would recognize that Prospero has gone too far in appropriating powers that should only belong to God and that therefore there was little choice for him but to relinquish his *rough magic* at the end of the play. The rhetorical effect of the claim, coming at the high point of his description of his skills, is offset by the danger of damnation implicit in his words.

2 *rough*

Either "crude or unrefined" or "severe or violent"

3 *their senses that / This airy charm is for*

The senses of those for whom this musical enchantment is created

4 *plummet sound*

Prospero will drown his books deeper than any *plummet* (a device to measure depth) can reach (*sound*).

5 *A solemn air, and the best comforter / To an unsettled fancy*

A solemn song, which is the best way to comfort a disturbed imagination

6 *Mine eyes, ev'n sociable to the show of thine, / Fall fellowly drops*

I.e., seeing you weep causes me to do the same

7 *ignorant fumes that mantle / Their clearer reason*

I.e., those forces that cloud their minds and keep them from thinking clearly

8 *pay thy graces / Home*

Repay your kindness fully

roots Have I made shake and, by the spurs,° plucked up
The pine and cedar; graves at my command
opened Have waked their sleepers,[1] oped,° and let 'em forth
By my so potent art. But this rough[2] magic   50
demanded I here abjure, and when I have required°
Some heavenly music, which even now I do,
purpose To work mine end° upon their senses that
This airy charm is for,[3] I'll break my staff,
many Bury it certain° fathoms in the earth,   55
And, deeper than did ever plummet sound,[4]
I'll drown my book.   *Solemn music.*

> *Here enters* **Ariel** *before, then* **Alonso**, *with a frantic ges-*
> *ture, attended by* **Gonzalo**; **Sebastian** *and* **Antonio** *in*
> *like manner, attended by* **Adrian** *and* **Francisco**. *They all*
> *enter the circle which* **Prospero** *had made, and there stand*
> *charmed, which* **Prospero** *observing, speaks:*

A solemn air, and the best comforter
To an unsettled fancy,[5] cure thy brains,
Now useless, boiled within thy skull. There stand,   60
For you are spell-stopped.
Holy Gonzalo, honorable man,
Mine eyes, ev'n sociable to the show of thine,
quickly Fall fellowly drops.[6] [*aside*] The charm dissolves apace,°
And as the morning steals upon the night,   65
Melting the darkness, so their rising senses
Begin to chase the ignorant fumes that mantle
Their clearer reason.[7]—O good Gonzalo,
gentleman My true preserver and a loyal sir°
To him thou follow'st, I will pay thy graces   70
Home[8] both in word and deed. [*to* **Alonso**] Most cruelly
Didst thou, Alonso, use me and my daughter.

1   *that entertained ambition, / Expelled remorse and nature*

    Who gave into his own ambition, forsaking compassion and natural love (for Prospero, as his brother)

2   *Their understanding / Begins to swell, and the approaching tide / Will shortly fill the reasonable shore*

    I.e., their understanding grows and their reason will soon be fully restored.

3   *hat and rapier*

    Necessary accessories for courtly attire

4   *As I was sometime Milan*

    I.e., as when I was Duke of Milan

conspirator Thy brother was a furtherer° in the act.

[*to* **Sebastian**] Thou art pinched for 't now, Sebastian.

[*to* **Antonio**] Flesh and blood,

You, brother mine, that entertained ambition, 75

who Expelled remorse and nature,¹ whom,° with Sebastian—

sufferings Whose inward pinches° therefore are most strong—

Would here have killed your King, I do forgive thee,

Unnatural though thou art. [*aside*] Their understanding

Begins to swell, and the approaching tide 80

Will shortly fill the reasonable shore²

There is not That now lies foul and muddy. Not° one of them

That yet looks on me or would know me.—Ariel,

Fetch me the hat and rapier³ in my cell.

undress I will discase° me and myself present 85

As I was sometime Milan.⁴ Quickly, spirit.   [**Ariel** *exits.*]

Thou shalt ere long be free.

[*Enter* **Ariel**.]

Ariel

[*sings*] Where the bee sucks, there suck I.

In a cowslip's bell I lie.

lie There I couch° when owls do cry. 90

On the bat's back I do fly

After summer merrily.

Merrily, merrily shall I live now

Under the blossom that hangs on the bough.

Prospero

Why, that's my dainty Ariel! I shall miss thee, 95

But yet thou shalt have freedom.—So, so, so.

Go to —To° the King's ship, invisible as thou art.

There shalt thou find the mariners asleep

1   *I drink the air before me*

    I.e., I will travel quickly. Ariel's expression is drawn from the Latin phrase *viam vorare*, or "I devour the way."

2   *Or ere*

    Before

3   *some enchanted trifle to abuse me, / As late I have been*

    A spirit or apparition to deceive me, as I have recently been deceived

4   *This must crave—— / An if this be at all— a most strange story.*

    This situation must have—if it is really happening at all, and is not an illusion—a very unusual story behind it.

5   *Thy dukedom I resign*

    I.e., I restore Milan to you. Alonso, as King of Naples, has the power to reinstate Prospero as the Duke of Milan.

deck Under the hatches.° The master and the boatswain
awakened / bring Being awake,° enforce° them to this place,   100
immediately And presently,° I prithee.

Ariel

I drink the air before me [1] and return
Or ere [2] your pulse twice beat.   *He exits.*

Gonzalo

All torment, trouble, wonder, and amazement
Lives Inhabits° here. Some heavenly power guide us   105
Out of this fearful country!

Prospero

                    [*to* **Alonso**] Behold, sir King,
The wrongèd Duke of Milan, Prospero.
For more assurance that a living prince
Does now speak to thee, I embrace thy body,
And to thee and thy company I bid   110
A hearty welcome.

Alonso

Whether   Whe'er° thou be'st he or no,
Or some enchanted trifle to abuse me,
As late I have been, [3] I not know. Thy pulse
Beats as of flesh and blood; and since I saw thee,
Th' affliction of my mind amends, with which,   115
I fear a madness held me. This must crave—
An if this be at all—a most strange story. [4]
Thy dukedom I resign [5] and do entreat
Thou pardon me my wrongs. But how should Prospero
Be living and be here?

Prospero

                    [*to* **Gonzalo**] First, noble friend,   120
elderly self Let me embrace thine age,° whose honor cannot
Be measured or confined.

1 *subtleties*

Illusions; devices. *Subtleties* were
also highly elaborate, sugary
desserts served at banquets;
Prospero likely puns on this
second meaning with his use of the
word *taste*.

2 *I here could pluck his Highness' frown*
upon you / And justify you traitors.

I.e., I could bring down the King's
displeasure upon you by proving
you traitors.

3 *perforce*

By necessity; Alonso has already
restored Prospero's dukedom, so
Antonio, *perforce*, must comply.

Gonzalo

                                        Whether this be
Or be not, I'll not swear.

Prospero

                                        You do yet taste
Some subtleties[1] o' th' isle that will not let you
Believe things certain. Welcome, my friends all.   125

pair   [*aside to* **Sebastian** *and* **Antonio**] But you, my brace° of
                lords, were I so minded,
I here could pluck his Highness' frown upon you
And justify you traitors.[2] At this time
I will tell no tales.

Sebastian

                        The devil speaks in him.

Prospero

                                                No.—
[*to* **Antonio**] For you, most wicked sir, whom to call   130
                brother
Would even infect my mouth, I do forgive

demand   Thy rankest fault, all of them, and require°
My dukedom of thee, which perforce,[3] I know,
Thou must restore.

Alonso

                        If thou be'st Prospero,

details   Give us particulars° of thy preservation,   135

ago   How thou hast met us here, whom three hours since°
Were wracked upon this shore, where I have lost—
How sharp the point of this remembrance is!—
My dear son Ferdinand.

Prospero

                                I am woe for 't, sir.

1   *her help, of whose soft grace / For the*
     like loss I have her sovereign aid, / And
     rest myself content

     I.e., the help of patience, whose
     compassion for my similar loss has
     helped me be at peace (with that loss)

2   *mudded in that oozy bed*

     I.e., buried in the mud at the
     bottom of the ocean

3   *they devour their reason and scarce*
     think / Their eyes do offices of the truth,
     their words / Are natural breath

     They have lost the ability to think
     clearly; they do not trust that their
     eyes reveal the truth or that their
     own words can be believed

Alonso

Irreparable is the loss, and patience   140

Says it is past her cure.

Prospero

                                        I rather think

You have not sought her help, of whose soft grace

For the like loss I have her sovereign aid,

And rest myself content. [1]

Alonso

                                        You the like loss?

Prospero

recent   As great to me as late,° and supportable   145

grievous To make the dear° loss have I means much weaker

Than you may call to comfort you—for I

Have lost my daughter.

Alonso

                                        A daughter?

O heavens, that they were living both in Naples,

The king and queen there! That they were, I wish   150

Myself were mudded in that oozy bed [2]

Where my son lies. When did you lose your daughter?

Prospero

In this last tempest.—I perceive these lords

wonder   At this encounter do so much admire°

That they devour their reason and scarce think   155

Their eyes do offices of truth, their words

Are natural breath. [3]—But, howsoe'er you have

Been jostled from your senses, know for certain

That I am Prospero and that very Duke

from   Which was thrust forth of° Milan, who most strangely   160

Upon this shore, where you were wracked, was landed

of   To be the lord on° 't. No more yet of this;

1   *'tis a chronicle of day by day, / Not a*
    relation for a breakfast, nor / Befitting
    this first meeting

    **I.e., it is a narrative to be told over
    time, not a report to be delivered
    quickly or one fit for this
    encounter**

2   *subjects none abroad*

    **I.e., no subjects elsewhere (only
    those within my cell)**

3   discovers

    **To *discover* on an early modern stage
    was to reveal characters previously
    unseen both by the audience and by
    those onstage; in all likelihood, this
    would be done by drawing back the
    curtain from the central opening in
    the tiring-house wall known as the
    discovery space (see Fig 3 on page 253).
    This is the last of the *wonders*
    Prospero sets up, though this time
    there is no magic required.**

4   chess

    **A game associated at the time with
    both the upper classes and with
    Mediterranean cultures, notably
    Spain and Italy, chess was often used
    as a metaphor for the maneuverings
    both of love and of politics: Stephen
    Orgel suggests that "[t]he territorial
    ambitions of their elders are
    transformed by Ferdinand and
    Miranda into the stratagems of
    chess"—which include cheating in
    order to acquire more kingdoms.
    Certainly it seems a little unsettling
    that the first time we see the young
    couple after their marriage they are
    engaged in symbolic and
    unscrupulous warfare.**

5   *for a score of kingdoms you should*
    wrangle, / And I would call it fair play

    And **may either carry the modern
    meaning or be used here as a
    variant of *an*, or "if." Therefore,
    Miranda may mean: (1) you would
    cheat me for twenty kingdoms, but
    because I love you I will swear you
    played honestly; (2) if I deemed it
    fair play, you would strive to win
    twenty kingdoms**

6   *compass thee about*

    Surround you

For 'tis a chronicle of day by day,

Not a relation for a breakfast, nor

Befitting this first meeting. [1] Welcome, sir;   165

This cell's my court. Here have I few attendants

And subjects none abroad. [2] Pray you, look in.

My dukedom since you have given me again,

repay   I will requite° you with as good a thing,

At least bring forth a wonder, to content ye   170

As much as me my dukedom.

     Here **Prospero** *discovers* [3] **Ferdinand** *and* **Miranda**

     playing at chess. [4]

Miranda

Sweet lord, you play me false.

Ferdinand

                  No, my dearest love,

I would not for the world.

Miranda

twenty   Yes, for a score° of kingdoms you should wrangle,

And I would call it fair play. [5]

Alonso

prove to be   If this prove°   175

illusion   A vision° of the island, one dear son

Shall I twice lose.

Sebastian

              A most high miracle!

Ferdinand

[*seeing* **Alonso** *and kneeling*] Though the seas threaten,

    they are merciful.

I have cursed them without cause.

Alonso

                 Now all the blessings

Of a glad father compass thee about. [6]   180

Arise and say how thou cam'st here.

1   *I am hers.*

    I will be Miranda's second father
    (as Prospero is to Ferdinand).

2   *ask my child forgiveness*

    Alonso feels he must ask Miranda's
    forgiveness for his part in her (and
    Prospero's) exile from Milan.

Miranda

O wonder!
How many goodly creatures are there here!
How beauteous mankind is! O brave new world
That has such people in 't!

Prospero

'Tis new to thee.

Alonso

[to **Ferdinand**] What is this maid with whom thou wast
at play?   185

longest Your eld'st° acquaintance cannot be three hours.
Is she the goddess that hath severed us
And brought us thus together?

Ferdinand

Sir, she is mortal;

divine But by immortal° providence she's mine.
I chose her when I could not ask my father   190

i.e., a father For his advice, nor thought I had one.° She
Is daughter to this famous Duke of Milan—

renowned; celebrated Of whom so often I have heard renown°
But never saw before—of whom I have
Received a second life; and second father   195
This lady makes him to me.

Alonso

I am hers. [1]
But, oh, how oddly will it sound that I
Must ask my child forgiveness. [2]

Prospero

There, sir, stop.
Let us not burden our remembrances with

sorrow A heaviness° that's gone.

1   *chalked forth the way*

    I.e., marked out the path

2   *Was Milan thrust from Milan that his*
    issue / Should become king of Naples?

    I.e., was Prospero exiled from
    Milan so that his descendants (i.e.,
    the children of Ferdinand and
    Miranda) could rule Naples?

3   *still embrace his heart / That*

    Always embrace the heart of
    anyone who

4   amazedly

    In a bewildered manner; with wonder

Gonzalo

inwardly   I have inly° wept,   200

Or should have spoke ere this. Look down, you gods,

And on this couple drop a blessèd crown,

For it is you that have chalked forth the way [1]

Which brought us hither.

Alonso

                                              I say amen, Gonzalo.

Gonzalo

Was Milan thrust from Milan that his issue   205

Should become kings of Naples? [2] Oh, rejoice

Beyond a common joy, and set it down

With gold on lasting pillars: in one voyage

Did Claribel her husband find at Tunis,

And Ferdinand, her brother, found a wife   210

i.e., found his   Where he himself was lost, Prospero his° dukedom

i.e., found ourselves   In a poor isle, and all of us ourselves°

own self   When no man was his own.°

Alonso

        [*to* **Ferdinand** *and* **Miranda**] Give me your hands.

Let grief and sorrow still embrace his heart

That [3] doth not wish you joy.

Gonzalo

                                              Be it so! Amen!   215

Enter **Ariel**, *with the* **Master** *and* **Boatswain**
amazedly [4] *following.*

Oh, look, sir; look, sir! Here is more of us.

I prophesied if a gallows were on land,

This fellow could not drown.

i.e., blasphemer   [*to* **Boatswain**] Now, blasphemy,°

1   *That swear'st grace o'erboard*

    **I.e., who caused God to abandon
    us by cursing**

2   *three glasses since*

    Three hours (*hourglasses*) ago

3   *gave out*

    reported

4   *tight and yare and bravely rigged*

    **Seaworthy, speedy, and with fine
    sails**

5   *clapped under hatches*

    Stashed below decks

6   *in all our trim*

    **I.e., dressed in all our garments.
    The phrase is often amended to
    "all her trim," which would then
    imply the ship, rather than the
    sailors, was all decked out.**

7   *Cap'ring to eye her*

    Dancing for joy to see her (the boat)

That swear'st grace o'erboard, [1] not an oath on shore?
Hast thou no mouth by land? What is the news?   220

Boatswain

The best news is that we have safely found
Our King and company. The next, our ship,
Which but three glasses since [2] we gave out [3] split,
Is tight and yare and bravely rigged [4] as when
We first put out to sea.

Ariel

                    [*aside to* **Prospero**] Sir, all this service   225
Have I done since I went.

Prospero

playful; resourceful   [*aside to* **Ariel**] My tricksy° spirit!

Alonso

increase   These are not natural events. They strengthen°
From strange to stranger. [*to* **Boatswain**] Say, how
    came you hither?

Boatswain

If I did think, sir, I were well awake,
I'd strive to tell you. We were dead of sleep,   230
And—how we know not—all clapped under hatches, [5]
diverse   Where but even now with strange and several° noises
Of roaring, shrieking, howling, jingling chains,
And more diversity of sounds, all horrible,
We were awaked, straightway at liberty,   235
Where we, in all our trim, [6] freshly beheld
Our royal, good, and gallant ship, our Master
Cap'ring to eye her. [7] On a trice, so please you,
separated   Even in a dream, were we divided° from them
bewildered   And were brought moping° hither.

1   *infest your mind with beating on*
     I.e., trouble your mind with
     persistent concerns about

2   *At picked leisure, / Which shall be*
     shortly, single I'll resolve you— / Which
     to you shall seem probable—of every /
     These happened accidents.
     I.e., soon, at a more leisurely time, I
     will privately give you a convincing
     explanation for all that has occurred.

3   *Every man shift for all the rest, and let no*
     man take care for himself
     In his drunken state, Stephano
     bungles the saying "every man for
     himself."

Ariel

[*aside to* **Prospero**] Was 't well done?   240

Prospero

[*aside to* **Ariel**] Bravely, my diligence. Thou shalt be free.

Alonso

This is as strange a maze as e'er men trod,

And there is in this business more than nature

director   Was ever conduct° of. Some oracle

Must rectify our knowledge.

Prospero

Sir, my liege,   245

Do not infest your mind with beating on [1]

The strangeness of this business. At picked leisure,

Which shall be shortly, single I'll resolve you—

Which to you shall seem probable—of every

These happened accidents. [2] Till when, be cheerful   250

And think of each thing well. [*aside to* **Ariel**] Come

   hither, spirit.

Set Caliban and his companions free;

Untie the spell.   [**Ariel** *exits.*]

[*to* **Alonso**] How fares my gracious sir?

There are yet missing of your company

Some few odd lads that you remember not.   255

Enter **Ariel** *driving in* **Caliban**, **Stephano**, *and*

Trinculo *in their stolen apparel.*

Stephano

Every man shift for all the rest, and let no man take care

Courage (Italian)   for himself, [3] for all is but fortune. *Coraggio*,°

gallant monster   bully-monster,° *coraggio!*

1   *If these be true spies which I wear in my head*

    I.e., if I can trust my eyes

2   *Mark but the badges of these men, my
    lords, / Then say if they be true.*

    **I.e., observe the emblems on their
    clothes, and then say if they are
    honest. Servants wore emblems of
    the house they served; Stephano
    and Trinculo are wearing stolen
    clothes, which means they are
    dishonest both for having stolen
    the clothes in the first place and for
    not displaying their affiliation with
    Alonso's household.**

3   *That could control the moon, make flows
    and ebbs*

    **I.e., that she (Sycorax) could
    control the moon and in doing so
    could also control the tides**

4   *deal in her command without her power*

    **I.e., wield the moon's power
    without her (the moon's) authority**

5   *know and own*

    I.e., acknowledge as yours

6   *had he*

    Did he get

Trinculo

If these be true spies which I wear in my head, [1] here's a

goodly sight.   260

Caliban

i.e., Sycorax's god / splendid   O Setebos,° these be brave° spirits indeed!

i.e., finely dressed   How fine° my master is! I am afraid

He will chastise me.

Sebastian

Ha, ha! What things are these, my lord Antonio?

Will money buy 'em?

Antonio

likely   Very like.° One of them   265

Is a plain fish and no doubt marketable.

Prospero

Mark but the badges of these men, my lords,

Then say if they be true. [2] [*indicating* **Caliban**] This

    misshapen knave,

His mother was a witch, and one so strong

That could control the moon, make flows and ebbs, [3]   270

And deal in her command without her power. [4]

These three have robbed me, and this demi-devil—

For he's a bastard one—had plotted with them

To take my life. Two of these fellows you

Must know and own. [5] This thing of darkness I   275

Acknowledge mine.

Caliban

                                    I shall be pinched to death.

Alonso

Is not this Stephano, my drunken butler?

Sebastian

He is drunk now. Where had he [6] wine?

1   *reeling ripe*

    I.e., so drunk that he staggers

2   *hath gilded 'em*

    I.e., flushed their faces

3   *I have been in such a pickle since I saw*
    you last that, I fear me, will never out of
    my bones. I shall not fear fly-blowing.

    I.e., I have been so thoroughly
    preserved by alcohol that will
    never leave my body and need not
    fear being infested with flies (as a
    decaying body would be).

4   *sirrah*

    Contemptuous term of address for
    one of inferior status

5   *a sore one*

    I.e., an inept one; also one in pain

Alonso

And Trinculo is reeling ripe. [1] Where should they

Find this grand liquor that hath gilded 'em? [2]   280

predicament —How cam'st thou in this pickle?°

Trinculo

I have been in such a pickle since I saw you last that, I

fear me, will never out of my bones. I shall not fear

fly-blowing. [3]

Sebastian

Why, how now, Stephano?   285

Stephano

Oh, touch me not! I am not Stephano, but a cramp.

Prospero

You'd be king o' th' isle, sirrah? [4]

Stephano

I should have been a sore one [5] then.

Alonso

[*indicating* **Caliban**] This is a strange thing as e'er I

looked on.

Prospero

He is as disproportioned in his manners   290

As in his shape. [*to* **Caliban**] Go, sirrah, to my cell;

desire Take with you your companions. As you look°

prepare To have my pardon, trim° it handsomely.

Caliban

Ay, that I will, and I'll be wise hereafter

forgiveness And seek for grace.° What a thrice-double ass   295

Was I to take this drunkard for a god

And worship this dull fool!

Prospero

                              Go to, away!

1   *luggage*

    I.e., the stolen clothing

2   *Take the ear*

    Captivate the listener

3   *draw near*

    I.e., go in; likely said as a directive to
    those exiting to Prospero's cell. It
    could also be said to the audience as
    Prospero prepares for the epilogue.

Alonso

[*to* **Stephano** *and* **Trinculo**] Hence, and bestow your
    luggage[1] where you found it.

                    [**Caliban**, **Stephano**, *and* **Trinculo** *exit.*]

Sebastian

Or stole it, rather.

Prospero

attendants   Sir, I invite your highness and your train°   300

To my poor cell, where you shall take your rest

while away   For this one night, which—part of it—I'll waste°

With such discourse as, I not doubt, shall make it

Go quick away: the story of my life

occurrences   And the particular accidents° gone by   305

Since I came to this isle. And in the morn

I'll bring you to your ship and so to Naples,

Where I have hope to see the nuptial

Of these our dear-belovèd solemnized;

And thence retire me to my Milan, where   310

Every third thought shall be my grave.

Alonso

                        I long

To hear the story of your life, which must

Take the ear[2] strangely.

Prospero

recount   I'll deliver° all,

And promise you calm seas, auspicious gales,

quick / catch up to   And sail so expeditious° that shall catch°   315

Your royal fleet far off.

(term of endearment)   [*aside to* **Ariel**] My Ariel, chick,°

That is thy charge. Then to the elements

Be free, and fare thou well!—Please you, draw near.[3]

                          They all exit.

1   Epilogue

The epilogue suggests Prospero's
perhaps surprising nervousness and
vulnerability at the end of the play,
dependent as he appears to be on the
audience's approval of his actions for
his return to Italy. Tiffany Stern,
though, in *Making Shakespeare*, argues
that prologues and epilogues were
generally spoken only once, at a
play's first performance, where the
audience by their applause or disdain
determined whether or not there
would ever be a second night; if this is
true, then interpretations of the play
that depend heavily on the epilogue
for understanding Prospero's
character and the play's ending are
arguably wide of the mark, though
this one seems so well suited to the
play's logic that it may well have been
the exception.

2   *bare island*

Both the empty stage and the
island Prospero inhabits

3   *release me from my bands / With the*
help of your good hands

I.e., release me from confinement
(in this role) with your applause

Epilogue [1]

Prospero

spells	Now my charms° are all o'erthrown,
	And what strength I have's mine own,
	Which is most faint. Now, 'tis true,
i.e., the audience	I must be here confined by you°
	Or sent to Naples. Let me not, 5
	Since I have my dukedom got
	And pardoned the deceiver, dwell
	In this bare island [2] by your spell,
	But release me from my bands
breeze (from clapping)	With the help of your good hands. [3] 10
	Gentle breath° of yours my sails
	Must fill, or else my project fails,
lack	Which was to please. Now I want°
	Spirits to enforce, art to enchant,
	And my ending is despair, 15
	Unless I be relieved by prayer,
	Which pierces so that it assaults
	Mercy itself and frees all faults.
sins	As you from crimes° would pardoned be,
favor	Let your indulgence° set me free. *He exits.* 20

245

THE
TEMPEST.

Actus primus, Scena prima.

A tempestuous noise of Thunder and Lightning heard: Enter a Ship-master, and a Botefwaine.

Mafter.

Ote-fwaine.

Botef. Heere Mafter: What cheere?

Maft. Good: Speake to th'Mariners: fall too't, yarely, or we run our felues a ground, beftirre, beftirre. *Exit.*

Enter Mariners.

Botef. Heigh my hearts, cheerely, cheerely my harts: yare, yare: Take in the toppe-fale: Tend to th'Mafters whiftle: Blow till thou burft thy winde, if roome enough.

Enter Alonfo, Sebaftian, Anthonio, Ferdinando, Gonzalo, and others.

Alon. Good Botefwaine haue care: where's the Mafter? Play the men.

Botef. I pray now keepe below.

Anth. Where is the Mafter, Bofon?

Botef. Do you not heare him? you marre our labour, Keepe your Cabines: you do afsift the ftorme.

Gonz. Nay, good be patient.

Botef. When the Sea is: hence, what cares thefe roarers for the name of King? to Cabine; filence: trouble vs not.

Gon. Good, yet remember whom thou haft aboord.

Botef. None that I more loue then my felfe. You are a Counfellor, if you can command thefe Elements to filence, and worke the peace of the prefent, wee will not hand a rope more, vfe your authoritie: If you cannot, giue thankes you haue liu'd fo long, and make your felfe readie in your Cabine for the mifchance of the houre, if it fo hap. Cheerely good hearts: out of our way I fay. *Exit.*

Gon. I haue great comfort from this fellow: methinks he hath no drowning marke vpon him, his complexion is perfect Gallowes: ftand faft good Fate to his hanging, make the rope of his deftiny our cable, for our owne doth little aduantage: If he be not borne to bee hang'd, our cafe is miferable. *Exit.*

Enter Botefwaine.

Botef. Downe with the top-Maft: yare, lower, lower, bring her to Try with Maine-courfe. *A cry within.* *Enter Sebaftian, Anthonio & Gonzalo.*

vpon this howling: they are lowder then the weather, or our office? yet againe? What do you heere? Shal we giue ore and drowne, haue you a minde to finke?

Sebaf. A poxe o'your throat, you bawling, blafphemous incharitable Dog.

Botef. Worke you then.

Anth. Hang cur, hang, you whorefon infolent Noyfemaker, we are leffe afraid to be drownde, then thou art.

Gonz. I'le warrant him for drowning, though the Ship were no ftronger then a Nutt-fhell, and as leaky as an vnftanched wench.

Botef. Lay her a hold, a hold, fet her two courfes off to Sea againe, lay her off.

Enter Mariners wet.

Mari. All loft, to prayers, to prayers, all loft.

Botef. What muft our mouths be cold?

Gonz. The King and Prince, at prayers, let's afsift them, for our cafe is as theirs.

Sebaf. I am out of patience.

An. We are meerly cheated of our liues by drunkards, This wide-chopt-rafcall, would thou mightft lye drowning the wafhing of ten Tides.

Gonz. Hee'l be hang'd yet,

Though euery drop of water fweare againft it, And gape at widft to glut him. *A confufed noyfe within.*

Mercy on vs.

We fplit, we fplit, Farewell my wife, and children, Farewell brother: we fplit, we fplit, we fplit.

Anth. Let's all finke with' King

Seb. Let's take leaue of him. *Exit.*

Gonz. Now would I giue a thoufand furlongs of Sea, for an Acre of barren ground: Long heath, Browne firrs, any thing; the wills aboue be done, but I would faine dye a dry death. *Exit.*

Scena Secunda.

Enter Profpero and Miranda.

Mira. If by your Art (my deereft father) you haue Put the wild waters in this Rore; alay them: The skye it feemes would powre down ftinking pitch, But that the Sea, mounting to th' welkins cheeke, Dafhes the fire out. Oh! I haue fuffered With thofe that I faw fuffer: A braue veffell

A   (Who

Editing *The Tempest*
by David Scott Kastan

The *Tempest* appears as the first play in the 1623 Folio, although it was one of the last that Shakespeare wrote (in 1611). Perhaps it was given pride of place in the volume because it was a late play that had not been printed previously (and so might be appealing to potential buyers), or merely because it was available in clean manuscript copy that made the printing easy. In any case, it is generally well printed, almost certainly from a manuscript prepared by Ralph Crane (one of six plays in the Folio identifiable as Crane's by certain idiosyncratic habits of composition, like the frequent dependence upon parentheses, the creation of unusual hyphenated words, and the use of group entries at the beginning of a scene of all characters who appear in it). The elaborate stage directions (see, for example, 4.1.138SD) are also characteristic of Crane and point to the fact that this was a text prepared primarily for the use of readers rather than actors.

In general, the editorial work for this present edition is a matter of normalizing spelling, capitalization, and punctuation, removing superfluous italics, regularizing the names of characters, rationalizing entrances and exits, and minor rewording and repositioning of stage directions. Comparison of the edited text of 1.1.1–1.2.6 with the facsimile page from the Folio (see opposite page) allows a reader to see the process. The speech prefixes are fully expanded, so the Folio's *Botes* is rendered **Boatswain**. Spelling throughout is modernized. As spelling in Shakespeare's time had not yet stabilized, words were spelled in various ways that indicated their proximate pronunciation, and compositors, in any case, were under no obligation to follow the spelling of their copy. Since for *The Tempest* the copy itself was produced by a scribe, the spelling of the printed Folio text is at least two removes from Shakespeare's own.

Little, then, is to be gained in an edition such as this by preserving the spelling of the original edition. Therefore, where in the seventh line on the facsimile page we find "toppe-sale," in a modernized text this becomes the familiar "topsail." Similarly, words like "Heere," "Cabine," and "lowder" unproblematically become "Here," "cabin," and "louder." Punctuation too is adapted to conform to modern practice (which is designed to clarify the logical relations between grammatical units, unlike seventeenth-century punctuation, which was dominated by rhythmical concerns), since the Folio punctuation is no more likely to be Shakespeare's own than is the spelling. Thus, at 1.1.18–21, the Boatswain says (in the Folio):

You are a Counsellor, if you can command these Elements to silence, and worke the peace of the present, wee will not hand a rope more, vse your authoritie:

Modernized this reads:

You are a councilor. If you can command these elements to silence and work the peace of the present, we will not hand a rope more. Use your authority.

Clarity is achieved at the expense of some loss of expressive detail, but normalizing spelling, capitalization, and punctuation allows the text to be read more or less as it was intended to be understood. Seventeenth-century readers would not have thought the Folio text in any sense quaint or archaic. The text would have seemed to them as modern as this one does to us. Modern readers, however, cannot help but be distracted by the different conventions of the Folio page. While it is indeed of interest to see how orthography and typography have changed over time, these are not the primary concerns of most readers of this edition, so what little is lost in careful modernization of the text is more than made up for by the removal of the artificial obstacle of unfamiliar spelling forms and punctuation practices that Shakespeare could never have intended to serve as interpretive difficulties for his readers.

Textual Notes

The list below records all substantive departures in this edition from the Folio text of 1623. It does not record modernizations of spelling and punctuation, expansions of abbreviations, corrections of obvious typographical errors, or adjustments of lineation. The adopted reading in this edition is given first in boldface followed by the original reading from the Folio. Editorial stage directions (SD) are not collated here but are enclosed within brackets in the text. Latin stage directions are translated (e.g., "They all exit" for "Exeunt omnes"), and the Latin act and scene indications of the Folio are similarly translated (e.g., "Act One, scene one" for "Actus primus, Scena prima").

List of Roles, [printed in the Folio at the end of the play]; **1.1.7SD Ferdinand** Ferdinando; **1.1.51 I'm** I'am; **1.1.57SP** [not in Folio]; **1.2.58 thou** [not in Folio]; **1.2.165 steaded** steeded; **1.2.173 princes** Princesse; **1.2.200 bowsprit** Bore-spritt; **1.2.229 Bermudas** Bermoothes; **1.2.282 she** he; **1.2.328 forth at** for that; **1.2.359 vile** vild; **1.2.383SP Spirits** [not in Folio]; **1.2.384SP Ariel** [not in Folio]; **1.2.385 Spirits** [not in Folio]; **1.2.405SP Spirits** [not in Folio]; **2.1.35SP Antonio** Seb;

2.1.36SP Sebastian Ant; 2.1.61; gloss glosses; 2.1.159 its it; 2.1.226
throes throwes; 2.2.9 mow moe; 2.2.61 at th' at'; 3.1.2 sets set;
3.1.15 busil'est busie lest; 3.2.117 scout cout; 3.3.2 ache akes; 3.3.29
islanders Islands; 3.3.33 human humaine; 3.3.65 plume plumbe;
4.1.9 of her her of; 4.1.13 gift guest; 4.1.74 Her here; 4.1.110SP Ceres
[not in Folio]; 4.1.193 them on on them; 4.1.229 Let 't let's; 5.1.20
human humane; 5.1.60 boiled boile; 5.1.72 Didst Did; 5.1.75 entertained entertaine; 5.1.82 lies ly; 5.1.257 *Coraggio* Coragio; 5.1.258
corragio Corasio

The Tempest on the Early Stage
by Gordon McMullan

We will never be able fully to re-create the original staging of Shakespeare's plays, but certain plays give more clues than others about the way in which they were first performed. *The Tempest* is one of those plays. It is both an astonishingly visual play and an astonishingly aural play. It has a strangeness and a theatrical intensity that stem from its practical need to convince its audience that clothes can be fresher and newer after a shipwreck than before, that spirits can disguise themselves as sea nymphs and circle the world in a moment, and that exiled monarchs can conjure up courtly dances and packs of hunting dogs from thin air. This need challenges and inspires directors now, just as it challenged and inspired Shakespeare's company in 1610. To look closely at the original conditions for performance is not simply to indulge in an act of speculative archaeology—it is to begin to understand why the play is what it is and to provide a basis for appreciating it not just as a fascinating printed text but as a practical stageplay with the ability to excite and amaze an audience.

Shakespeare's London offered an astonishingly—perhaps a uniquely—intense and varied theatrical environment. Company

Fig 1. In the large London playhouses, the balcony above the stage could be used for staging, seating, or to house musicians.

Fig 2. English Renaissance drama made minimal use of sets or backdrops. In the absence of a set, the stage pillars could be incorporated into the action, standing in for trees and other architectural elements.

Fig 3. The discovery space, located in the middle of the backstage wall, could be used as a third entrance as well as a location for scenes requiring special staging, such as in a tomb or bedchamber.

Fig 4. A trapdoor led to the area below the stage, known as "Hell" (as contrasted with the painted ceiling, known as "Heaven" or the "heavens"). Ghosts or other supernatural figures could descend through the trap, and it could also serve as a grave.

competed with company, and the audiences had their pick of theaters to attend. Shakespeare wrote his plays for the company in which he had a financial interest, the Lord Chamberlain's Men, who acquired royal patronage to become the King's Men under James I in 1603. The company, by far the most successful acting troupe in London, consisted of a total of fifteen or so men and four or five boys, the former performing a full range of roles but generally playing to type since the playwright was also one of their number and knew their abilities and styles intimately, the latter playing the roles of women and children and being, as far as we can tell, no less talented than the adult actors. In addition, there would have been extras of various kinds, along with a backstage staff including a scribe and a prompter. The company (like all acting companies in this period) performed with astonishing regularity, putting on a different play most afternoons and never playing runs: popular plays were repeated, but the actors kept a repertory of twenty or thirty established plays in their heads and added new ones as they were written, keeping them going if they were successful. Audiences had a key role in determining the success of a given play: if they withheld their applause on the first night, then that play was simply dropped and never performed again. Moreover, they saw plays in more repertories than just that of the King's Men and so were actively involved in obliging the different companies to keep an eye on what was successful elsewhere and find ways to adapt newly popular plots, motifs, and styles for their own repertory.

The Tempest, as it happens, had a wider range of audiences than most plays in the Shakespeare canon, since it seems to have been written for and performed at no fewer than three distinct venues: the court, the Globe, and the Blackfriars. The first performances of the play for which we have a record both took place at Whitehall—that is, at James I's court—but the King's Men habitually brought to court plays that they had established first of all in their own theatrical repertory, and there is no need to treat the play (as some critics have done) as something written specifically for the court, as a kind of command performance isolated from the commercial context of public performance. Still, it is useful to remember that one of the first people to see this play of politics, usurpation, conspiracy, and rebellion was the King himself. Moreover, this particular performance of *The Tempest* may have benefited from props and scenery left over from a court masque such as *Oberon*, which had been performed less than a year earlier and featured a coastline, a cave, and rocks, and could thus have furnished the visuals of the island—though, since scenery was never used in the theaters at this period, it is perhaps unlikely that it would have been incorporated for just one performance.

With or without actual painted scenery, *The Tempest* is, as we have noted, a play that calls for a range of visual and aural effects. The key scenes of shipwreck, banquet, and masque share a spectacular, magical quality that depends upon careful staging, and the figures of Caliban and Ariel require distinct costuming and cosmetic work. Special effects abound. For the storm scene alone, there must have been thunder machines (cannonballs rolled in a metal trough), a wind machine (flapping canvas on a wheel), and the crack of fireworks simulating lightning. And for virtually every other scene, music is required, either for the eerie noises of the isle or as accompaniment to songs. These effects seem to call for a theatrical environment a little different from that offered by the Globe.

This should come as no surprise, because *The Tempest* was first performed at a time of major change for the company, as they extended their operations beyond the Globe by beginning to play at a second, smaller, more intimate theater inside the city walls. All of Shakespeare's plays to this point had been written for performance at the Globe or its predecessors—that is, for a large, round (or polygonal), open-air space with both standing room and galleried seating for auditors of different income levels. But the company had for years owned another theater—an indoor theater with a rather different layout—without being able actually to use it. James Burbage had had this other theater constructed for the company—inside the ancient monastic hall of the Blackfriars—back in 1596, but his plans were ambushed by local residents disinclined to share their neighborhood with a playhouse, and there had been no option but to lease it out until circumstances changed.

This second theater, finally reclaimed by the company in 1608 (though not, because of enforced plague closures, used until 1610), was a space very different indeed from the open-air amphitheater in which they had played since 1599: it was half the size (and its stage was a third the size); it housed a noticeably smaller audience and charged noticeably more for entry, thus creating a more uniform and privileged set of auditors, all of whom (unlike a good proportion of the audience at the Globe) were seated; and performances there were mainly lit not by daylight but by candlelight. The effect of this seems to have been the production of plays noticeably different from those experienced in the Globe or any other open-air space: the stage was tight and intense, the cast close up both to each other and to the audience (a few of whom actually sat on edges of the stage), the music more focused and emotionally manipulative, the visual experience wholly different not only because the atmosphere must have been thick with candle smoke but also because the darkness made lighting effects (boosting candlepower with mirrors, for instance) a valuable addition to the staging. Changes of this sort were inevitably going to have an effect on the kinds of plays being written for the company by Shakespeare and others.

Unsurprisingly, then, the King's Men's reoccupation of the Blackfriars appears to coincide with a distinct change in style in Shakespeare's output—he began to write what we know as his late plays at this time—and, though, of course, there may have been other contingencies functioning to provoke these changes, it is generally assumed that the new venue helped shape the new style. Not that

Shakespeare stopped writing for the Globe: we know, for instance, that Henry VIII, a later play than The Tempest and one that, while it has the title and trappings of a history play, clearly resembles the late plays in a series of ways large and small, was performed at the Globe rather than the Blackfriars on at least one occasion, because in June 1613 an accident in the course of a performance of this play led to the burning down of the company's main theater. But we know from Dryden's preface to the adaptation he and Davenant developed from The Tempest in 1667 that it had been "acted with success" at the Blackfriars when first played. And it displays certain internal clues—more than does any other play in the Shakespeare canon—that suggest performance in the more intimate, enclosed space this theater offered: the scenes of masque and banquet, the lack of crowd scenes or battles, and the limited number of characters on stage at one time, plus perhaps some acrobatic "flying" from Ariel by way of ladders or trapezes of various kinds, which would have been more practical in a roofed space with shadows than in an open-air amphitheater. Two clues in particular make the case: the first is the centrality of music to the play in performance, the second the clarity of the play's five-act structure.

Dramatic structure might seem an odd way of locating a play in a particular theatrical space, but the logic is straightforward. In the Globe and other outdoor theaters of the period, natural light illuminated both stage and audience; plays were performed in daylight, and even if it rained, most of the audience (all except the groundlings) were under roofs. But in the Blackfriars there was limited natural light (the number and size of windows remains a matter of debate) and illumination, as we have seen, came from candles—hundreds of candles. These candles needed trimming (the candles themselves replacing, wax removing from the trays into which they dripped) roughly every half hour or so, that is, about three times during a play. Thus the birth—or at least the consolidation—of the act break and, in due course, of the modern-day intermission.

As for music and sound effects, there are certain essentials that inevitably make *The Tempest* distinctive in performance, then and now: not only a full-tilt storm scene at the start, but also a series of noises (jangling, confused, or misleading), some ethereal offstage music, and the sound of hunting horns and barking hounds. The Blackfriars came complete with a skilled company of musicians, and it is clear both that music became a more clearly integral part of performance than it had been before and that that music was quieter (strings and woodwind rather than brass and drums) than in the open-air theaters. The Blackfriars also housed an organ, which could have been used to eerie effect for an island "full of noises." In fact, the entire aural experience would have been different: at the Globe, for instance, noises beyond the theater's walls would have been intrusive in a way that they would not in the indoor playhouse.

As centuries of successful performances of the play have shown, Prospero's island can be created in the most unlikely of spaces, whether indoors or outdoors, silent or noisy. Our understanding of the play does not depend upon our knowledge of how it was first performed. But we can imagine *The Tempest* in its first performances taking place in a specific theatrical space in certain specific conditions that were a little different from those Shakespeare had in mind when writing, say, *Hamlet* or *Othello*. And while that awareness ought not to restrict our sense of the theatrical possibilities of the play, it perhaps helps provide a basis on which to understand the decisions modern directors make in carving out performances that both sustain and renew those early experiences.

Significant Performances
by Gordon McMullan

1611   First recorded performance at Whitehall before the King and court on Hallowmas Night. Nothing is known of the nature of the performance, though critics have speculated that the players might have made use of scenery originally constructed for a court masque: since scenery was never used on the professional stage at the time this seems highly unlikely but not impossible.

1613   Second recorded performance at Whitehall as part of celebrations marking the wedding of King James's daughter Elizabeth to Frederick, Elector Palatine, the principal Protestant ruler of Germany, in the first of James's projected weddings-for-peace—his plan being to marry his daughter and two sons to Protestant and Catholic princelings across Europe and thereby reduce conflict between nations. Thirteen plays were performed for the wedding, including four (*Much Ado About Nothing, Othello,* and *The Winter's Tale,* as well as *The Tempest*) by Shakespeare.

1667   First revival after the theaters reopened at the Restoration; the text performed is a new version by Davenant and Dryden called *The Tempest, or The Enchanted Isle,* which includes only a third or so of Shakespeare's text. Prospero's role is substantially diminished,

Antonio is downplayed, and Sebastian disappears; Caliban's part is reduced and Ariel's increased; Miranda has a sister, Dorinda, and Caliban a twin sister, Sycorax. Prospero also has a foster son, Hippolito, who embodies the sexual innocence that is Miranda's sole preserve in Shakespeare's play. This revision of the play is the one that most audiences saw for nearly two hundred years—which is not atypical, since all but a handful of Shakespeare's plays were performed in heavily reworked versions from the late seventeenth to the early nineteenth centuries.

1674 Operatic version of the play by Thomas Shadwell (though more, in our sense, like a Bollywood movie than an opera, with spoken dialogue interrupted by song-and-dance sequences), first performed at Duke's Theatre, London, with music by a series of composers including, for a later revision, Henry Purcell. Popular for decades, the opera was based on the Davenant and Dryden adaptation and involved complex stage machinery and a great deal of trapeze-based flying on the part of Ariel.

1757 First sustained production of Shakespeare's, rather than Davenant's, text (though there were still cuts, especially in Act Two, scene one), presented by the actor-manager David Garrick at the Drury Lane Theatre, London, and occasionally revived over a fifty-year period. The previous year Garrick had offered his own operatic version, but it was not successful.

1789 Version by John Philip Kemble at Drury Lane, restoring much of the Davenant-Dryden-Shadwell material, including the characters of Dorinda and Hippolito. Popular for over a decade, this version was revived every year during Kemble's period of management.

1806 New version by Kemble, this time at the rival Covent Garden Theatre. Kemble played Prospero in a production that was still based on Davenant's plot but with much less operatic material, and which became the standard acting version of the play for twenty or more years. Critics were beginning to call for the original text, but audiences were happy for a while longer with derivatives of the Davenant-Dryden adaptation.

1838 Shakespeare's text, with only minimal additions, was revived by William Charles Macready at Covent Garden, with Macready as Prospero, Helen Faucit as Miranda, and a particularly perky and acrobatic Ariel played by Priscilla Horton. This version retained some of the music from the operatic *Tempest* but dispensed with Dorinda, Hippolito, and the rest of the added characters; it was noticeable perhaps above all for the complexity of its staging and special effects.

1847 Production by Samuel Phelps at Sadler's Wells, London, with less than the usual quantity of scenic effects and machines, which was praised for its emphasis on Shakespeare's text. It was, all the same, fairly heavily cut, and it incorporated a range of special effects, notably of magic flames, thus remaining within the spectacular tradition.

1857 Production by Charles Kean at Covent Garden, generally referred to as an "extravaganza" and notable for its spectacular excess, with much dependence on large-scale painted scenery, including a full-scale storm scene as prologue, a tableau of flying spirits, and dances of fauns and satyrs. It concluded by bringing on an apparently life-size ship to bear Prospero home. With all these scenic additions, the production ran for a full four hours even with Kean cutting away at the text in rehearsal.

1891   Production by Frank Benson for the Stratford Festival at the Memorial Theatre, with Benson playing Caliban as the play's central role. His ideas for the part were based on the Darwinian idea of the "missing link" between animals and humans, and he played on all fours, entering with a real fish between his teeth. Partly due to a lack of funding, Benson created a simpler *Tempest* than was usual, omitting the opening storm scene, for instance. He nonetheless echoed Kean's staging in several places, incorporating lavish ballet sequences, and seems to have hankered after a large-scale show.

1897   Production by William Poel for the Elizabethan Stage Society, performed with no scenery and only simple, unoperatic music. Poel was well known for producing a series of Shakespeare plays in as near as possible to "original" conditions, that is, with minimal sets (though with elaborate Elizabethan-style costumes), little spectacle, and a firm emphasis on the words. This production thus marked a clear break with the dominant tradition of elaborately staged *Tempests*.

1904   Production by Herbert Beerbohm Tree at His Majesty's Theatre, London, that revived the traditional emphasis on elaborate staging. Tree echoed Benson by playing Caliban as a Darwinian primitive but gave the character a noble sensitivity, expanding the role with extended dance sequence and leaving him dumbly bereft at the end, watching the ship sail away. Tree, who revived a range of Shakespeare plays in the last years of Victorian spectacular theater, gave a nod to the future in this production by making particular use of new electrical lighting technology rather than painted scenery.

1908   Twelve-minute-long silent film version, directed by Percy Stow. The film featured location shots and split-screen effects and demonstrated, at the start of the movie era, a cinematic potential for the play that has yet to be fulfilled, even in the innovative films of Jarman and Greenaway.

1914 Production by Ben Greet at London's Old Vic Theatre that harked back to the experiments of Poel in its lack of special scenic effects and the brevity of its performance, which lasted just two hours. On the other hand, Greet incorporated an opening ballet of spirits and, in line with the established tradition of having women play the part of Ariel, cast a young Sybil Thorndike as Ferdinand, thus demonstrating a continued relationship with the operatic line.

1930 Production by Harcourt Williams at the Old Vic starring, as Prospero and Caliban respectively, John Gielgud and Ralph Richardson, two of the three most prominent English stage stars of the twentieth century (the third being Laurence Olivier) performing together for the first time. Gielgud was only twenty-six at the time, so his performance challenged the received idea that Prospero must be old: he went on to play the part several more times, until he himself was in old age. This production also marked the first time in two hundred years that Ariel was played by a man, the dancer Leslie French.

1934 Production by Tyrone Guthrie at the Old Vic, starring Charles Laughton as Prospero (in a manner considered overly reminiscent of Father Christmas by one reviewer, who hated the production) and returning Ariel's part to a woman, Elsa Lanchester, who played it in an overtly feminine manner and in Art Deco costume.

1945 Production by Margaret Webster at the Alvin Theater, New York, for the Theater Guild, with Canada Lee as the first black actor to play Caliban: his costume emphasized the character's supposed human/fish hybridity.

1954 Production by Robert Helpmann at the Old Vic with Michael Hordern as a bitter Prospero, resenting his exile and bent on revenge, in a manner that broke firmly with the tradition of portraying Prospero as benign and serene.

1956 *The Forbidden Planet*, cult science-fiction film based on *The Tempest*, located on a planet where Dr. Morbius is conducting experiments and his daughter, Altaira, falls for a visiting spaceman from Earth. The danger posed by an invisible force (the film's equivalent of Caliban) turns out, in a Freudian *coup*, to be a projection of Morbius's psyche only evaded by his death. *The Forbidden Planet* was the first film to feature an entirely electronic score.

1957 Psychoanalytically inspired production by Peter Brook at Stratford. John Gielgud played Prospero once again, this time as a depressed and isolated man in exile whose internal turmoil shapes the island as a grim dreamscape of caves and undergrowth, but who nonetheless, by the last act, in Gielgud's words, "goes back to his dukedom as a kind of God."

1968 Experimental production by Peter Brook at the Roundhouse, London, mostly mimed, drawing again on psychoanalytic ideas to emphasise the play's repressed sexual energy and violence. Sycorax appeared on stage, giving birth to evil in the shape of Caliban, and Prospero finished the play sooner than expected, as if uninterested in proceedings once Miranda and Ferdinand's marriage had taken place.

1970 Production by Jonathan Miller at the Mermaid, London, reading the play—on the basis of Octave Mannoni's *Prospero and Caliban*—as a dramatization of the end of empire and of colonialism's ongoing consequences for the ex-colony. Prospero became a colonial governor at the point of handover to the indigenous people, represented by Ariel as high-caste servant and Caliban as low-caste worker. The conclusion of the play suggested that Ariel, who picks up Prospero's staff, is about to echo colonial structures by oppressing Caliban.

1974 Production by Peter Hall for the National Theatre at the Old Vic, influenced by Stephen Orgel and Roy Strong's recently published book on the masque and staged in Jacobean style, with Gielgud (again) as Prospero costumed this time as a cross between the masque designer Inigo Jones and the magician John Dee.

1978 Production by Giorgio Strehler at the Teatro Lirico, Milan, with the actors of the Piccolo Teatro, emphasising the Italianness of the play through the use of *commedia dell'arte* features. It was in several ways a harking back to the spectacular tradition despite its modern appearance, lasting four hours and dependent upon the audience's recognition of a direct connection between Prospero as on-stage controller of the action and Strehler's role as director of the play.

1980 Iconoclastic gay film version by Derek Jarman, emphasizing the play's sexual possibilities. Prospero (Heathcote Williams) is portrayed as a tyrannical magician manipulating the other characters, and Miranda (the alternative pop singer Toyah Willcox) as a childish sophisticate flouncing round the empty mansion they inhabit, unfazed by the threat of Jack Birkett's effetely cruel Caliban. Ariel is a rebel, damaged by Sycorax and overtly resenting Prospero's power. The film concludes with a magnificently camp masque line-danced by sailors to the jazz song "Stormy Weather," sung by larger-than-life diva Elisabeth Welsh, looking like she's having the time of her life.

1991   *Prospero's Books*, a film version of *The Tempest* lavishly directed by Peter Greenaway with an extravagant set, exaggerated costumes, and generally striking visuals (including a surreal book-by-book account of Prospero's library, echoing Borges). The text itself is heavily cut to ensure that Prospero—a powerful but benign figure played for the last time by Gielgud—remains central, speaking all the major speeches, not just his own. Naked balletic figures swirl through the scenes; Ariel is a little boy peeing from a swing; and Caliban is played with sinuous and malevolent physicality by dancer Michael Clark (thereby echoing the earlier casting of dancers in the role of Ariel). This is the spectacular tradition transformed to celluloid.

1993   Production by Sam Mendes for the Royal Shakespeare Company at Stratford, presented with minimal staging (except, by contrast, for a masque scene designed like a Victorian toyshop) and notable above all for Simon Russell Beale's wholly convincing portrayal of a resentful Ariel, spitting in Prospero's face before departing at the end of the play—a piece of business that sufficiently outraged reviewers that it was withdrawn for later performances.

1995   Two productions in the United States: one by Ron Daniels for the American Repertory Theater in Cambridge, Massachusetts, echoing Greenaway but incorporating a colonial reading; the other by George C. Wolfe for the Shakespeare Festival in Central Park, New York. Taking a hint from *Forbidden Planet*, it cast *Star Trek: Next Generation* star Patrick Stewart—who was a successful Shakespearean actor before taking up the role of Captain Picard—as a furious Prospero. Described by one critic as "the busiest *Tempest* in history," this production stressed the multiculturalism of the island and emphasized racial division rather than reconciliation.

Inspired by *The Tempest*

Since its first performance in or around 1611, *The Tempest* has continually enchanted audiences, becoming one of Shakespeare's most perennially popular plays. Yet *The Tempest* is not only an imaginative tale about the transformative power of art and magic—it is also and equally a parable of political domination, an archetypal story of parent-child dynamics, and an allegory of moral and ethical education. Over the years, many artists have discovered "rich and strange" material in Shakespeare's play. In their dramatic, cinematic, musical, and literary adaptations, these artists articulate and emphasize particular elements of Shakespeare's story and style, spinning the raw stuff of *The Tempest* in countless new directions.

Stage

The first adaptation of *The Tempest*, William Davenant and John Dryden's *The Tempest, or the Enchanted Isle*, premiered in 1667. Like many Restoration adapters, Davenant and Dryden took Shakespeare's original text and rewrote large sections of it, adding and deleting dialogue, characters, and subplots at will in order to improve what they considered to be the play's artistic flaws in terms

of the aesthetic norms of their own time. In the interest of impos-
ing a more formal symmetry upon the plot, for example, Miranda
was given a younger sister, Dorinda, and Prospero was given a foster
son, Hippolito, who lives on the other side of the island and who,
at the outset of the play, has never seen a woman—just as his un-
known foster sisters, Miranda and Dorinda, have never seen a man.
The happy ending of the play results in two couples: Miranda and
Ferdinand, and Dorinda and Hippolito. In further examples of symmetry, Sycorax is transformed into Caliban's twin, and Ariel is given
a companion spirit, Milcha. _The Tempest; or the Enchanted Isle_ became an
immediate hit and stayed popular through the eighteenth century,
though usually in Thomas Shadwell's musical adaptation performed
first in 1674. The unusual popularity of this version led to a spoof,
Thomas Duffet's _The Mock Tempest_, produced by the King's Company in
1675. Instead of living on a deserted island, Prospero, Miranda, and
Dorinda are incarcerated in Bridewell prison, with the storm that
opens Shakespeare's play re-imagined as a brothel riot.

Several later _Tempest_ adaptations shifted focus away from
Prospero and his family, putting Shakespeare's "savage and deformed
slave," Caliban, in a newly central role. Ernest Renan's philosophical
1878 closet drama (that is, a play written to be read rather than
performed) _Caliban: Suite de le Tempête_ draws on the theories of Charles
Darwin to depict Caliban as a character who undergoes a moral
evolution. Presented as a sequel to Shakespeare's _The Tempest_, Renan's
drama has Caliban and Ariel following Prospero and the others to
Milan. There, the drunkard Caliban stages a coup and becomes the
ruler of Milan. Once King, however, Caliban abandons his dissolute
ways and imitates the moral behavior of Prospero.

Percy MacKaye's masque drama _Caliban by the Yellow Sands_
also focused its attentions on Caliban, and the ways in which
he represents the human potential for change and growth. The
massive pageant was produced in 1916 as part of an extensive series

of celebrations, both British and American, marking Shakespeare's tercentenary. A bona fide extravaganza, _Caliban by the Yellow Sands_ was originally performed in New York's Lewisohn Stadium over ten nights by a cast of 1,500 performers (including an uncredited Isadora Duncan), for audiences of nearly 135,000 people. MacKaye's masque used the characters and, to a lesser extent, the plot conditions of _The Tempest_ to offer an allegorical depiction of an individual's moral education. It begins with Prospero's arrival on the island, his killing of the witch Sycorax, and his freeing of Ariel (who had been imprisoned inside an idol of the pagan god Setebos). With Ariel and Miranda's help, Prospero turns his attentions to Sycorax's son, Caliban. In an attempt to dismantle the sorceress's evil influence and turn her son toward the path of righteousness, Prospero produces a pageant for Caliban, composed of elaborate, edifying scenes from various plays by Shakespeare. Though the process is not a smooth one, Caliban eventually becomes reformed and enlightened as a result of this cultural exposure.

The 1969 play _Une Tempête_ (_A Tempest_), by Aime Cesare of Martinique, de-emphasizes Shakespeare's romantic themes and intra-European political struggles in favor of a frank exploration of the master/slave dynamic. In this study of the contemporary aftermath of colonization, Prospero is depicted as a decadent, power-hungry European, while Caliban is transformed into an articulate African field hand and Ariel into a mulatto house servant. Shakespeare's music is replaced with slave songs and spirituals, and the Yoruba trickster god, Eshu, is called in to bless the marriage of the young lovers. Cesaire wrote _Une Tempête_ to be performed by an all-black cast, and in a prologue to the play the Master of Ceremonies distributes masks to the actors in order to facilitate their playing of white Europeans. At the end of the play, Caliban—whose rebellion against his oppressors has failed—draws on this image of an externalized identity when he rails, "Prospero, you are a great illusionist:

deception knows you well. And you have lied to me so much, lied about the world, about myself, that you finally imposed an image on me, an image of myself, an 'underdeveloped' you say, an 'under achiever,' that is how you have made me see myself, and I hate this image! It is false!"

Film

The 1956 sci-fi movie *The Forbidden Planet* follows J. J. Adams (played by Leslie Nielsen), the captain of a spaceship that lands on the planet Altair-IV. There, Adams and his crew find Professor Morbius, his daughter Altaira, and their robot Robby (i.e., Ariel). In place of Prospero's magic, Professor Morbius wields the power of advanced, alien science. In the film, the violent presence of Shakespeare's Caliban is reimagined as an invisible electromagnetic force that damages Adams's ship. It is eventually revealed that the power charge was a manifestation of Morbius's repressed anger and jealousy at the growing affections between the captain and his daughter.

The basic premise of *The Forbidden Planet* was revived in Bob Carlton's 1981 comic rock musical *Return to the Forbidden Planet*. In this version, the dashing space captain Tempest arrives on the planet D'Illyria (a nod to Shakespeare's *Twelfth Night*), home to Doctor Prospero and his beautiful daughter Miranda. The two have been living in isolation ever since Prospero's wife, Gloria, tricked them into banishment in order to gain control of a top-secret formula Prospero was developing—a formula that transforms thoughts into reality. As the love-struck Miranda attempts to catch the attention of Captain Tempest, a multi-tentacled monster begins attacking the ship. As in *Forbidden Planet*, the monster is revealed to be a manifestation of Prospero's consciousness and so, in order to save the crew, the mad doctor sacrifices himself. *Return to the Forbidden Planet* features a soundtrack comprised of classic rock songs, such as "Good Vibrations," "Teenager in Love," and "The Monster Mash."

In Paul Mazursky's loose adaptation, *The Tempest* (1982), the political intrigue that sets Shakespeare's plot in motion is transformed into a personal, domestic dispute. Frustrated by his failing relationship with his wife, Antonio, who is having an affair with his boss (a tycoon named Alonzo), middle-aged architect Philip Dimitrius (John Cassavetes) flees New York City with his teenage daughter, Miranda (Molly Ringwald), in tow. Settling on a lush, deserted Greek island, Philip passes the time with his daughter, his charming mistress Aretha (Susan Sarandon), and an eccentric local goatherd named Kalibanos (Raul Julia). The storm that opens Shakespeare's play is transposed to the climax of Mazursky's film and shipwrecks Antonia, Alonzo, and various secondary characters on the island. Philip comes to realize the mistake he made in abandoning Antonia and, like Prospero and Antonio before them, husband and wife reconcile at the film's conclusion.

The most famous recent adaptation of *The Tempest* is Peter Greenaway's film *Prospero's Books* (1991). This surreal fantasy uses animation, mirror images, and various camera tricks to represent the effects of Prospero's magic. In the film, the play *The Tempest* is Prospero's own creation, written with help from the books he brought with him into exile. As he writes the play, Prospero (played by the eminent Shakespearean actor John Gielgud) speaks the other characters' dialogue aloud. The film ends with Ariel interrupting Prospero's writing process and wresting away control of the manuscript, scripting his master's turn to mercy in Act Five, scene one. Angered, Prospero stops writing and throws his books into the sea. Caliban rescues two of the books: *Thirty-Six Plays* by William Shakespeare and Prospero's script of *The Tempest*.

Other recent, idiosyncratic film adaptations include Derek Jarman's experimental *Tempest* (1979), an intensely imagistic film featuring a clear homosexual undercurrent and a strong punk rock sensibility, and Jack Bender's 1998 TV movie, also called *The Tempest*, set on the slave plantations of a pre-Civil War Mississippi Bayou.

Poetry

The Tempest has an extraordinarily extensive afterlife in poetry. One
of the most significant poems inspired by Shakespeare's play is W. H.
Auden's 1944 *The Sea and the Mirror*, subtitled "A Commentary on Shakespeare's *The Tempest*." Written in the midst of World War II, this long
poem is conceived as a series of dramatic monologues spoken by the
various characters of *The Tempest*. It begins in a theater following a performance of the play, where the magician, in a touching, unrhymed
section titled "Prospero to Ariel," bids farewell to his faithful servant
and looks ahead mournfully to his future in Milan. After the other
characters deliver their poetic speeches—in a staggering variety of
verse forms, including a beautifully evocative villanelle for Miranda—
the poem closes with a prose monologue titled "Caliban to the Audience," in which Caliban addresses the contemporary reader directly on
the topic of art.

Several other famous poets have reworked material from
The Tempest, including Percy Bysshe Shelley ("With a Guitar: To Jane,"
1822), Robert Browning ("Caliban upon Setebos," 1864), Rainer Maria
Rilke ("The Spirit Ariel," 1921), H.D. ("By Avon River," 1949), Sylvia Plath
("Ariel," 1965), and Ted Hughes ("Setebos," included in 1998's *Birthday
Letters*, Hughes's account of his marriage to Plath).

As in other artistic genres, many contemporary poets who
have been drawn to *The Tempest* come from non-European nations.
Lemuel Johnson of Sierra Leone, for example, titled his 1973 book of
poetry *Highlife for Caliban*. Indian-born Suniti Namjoshi's 1989 poem
sequence "Snapshots of Caliban" reimagines Caliban as a female figure, and Miranda's lesbian lover besides. In his 1971 book *Frantz Fanon's
Uneven Ribs*, Ugandan Taban lo Liyong identifies himself with Caliban,
cursing in a language that is not his own, and in Barbados, Edward
Kamau Brathwaite published the influential poems "Caliban" (1969)
and "Letter Sycorax" (1993).

Novels

Gloria Naylor's *Mama Day* (1988) takes place alternately in New York City and Willow Springs, an island off the coast of South Carolina and Georgia. The matriarch of Willow Springs, an old black midwife with magical powers, is named Miranda "Mama" Day. The novel centers on the tragic relationship between Mama Day's great-niece Ophelia "Cocoa" Day and a New York-bred man named George Andrews. *Mama Day* draws on *The Tempest* for its magical, mysterious island setting, and the character of Mama Day represents a melding and re-imagining of three central Shakespearean characters: Miranda (in her name), Prospero (in her magical abilities), and Caliban (in her legacy as a descendant of slaves). In *Mama Day*, the power that had been identified in *The Tempest* with white, male Europeans is vested in a black woman, upending the power dynamic of Shakespeare's play.

In her 1992 novel *Indigo*, or *Mapping the Waters*, the British writer Marina Warner restores Caliban's mother, Sycorax, to a central position within the *Tempest* tale. Sycorax is a seventeenth-century sorceress living on a Caribbean island, who rescues a slave's infant son from drowning and raises the boy—Caliban—as her own. She eventually adopts a second child, an infant Arawak Indian girl named Ariel, and establishes a compound for herself and her family on one end of the island. When the British Kit Everard arrives on the scene, seeking to make his fortune from the island's bounties of indigo and sugar, Sycorax's children become inextricably involved with the colonizers: Caliban as the leader of a rebellious uprising, and Ariel as Everard's lover and the mother of his child. Warner's seventeenth-century narrative is intertwined with a twentieth-century one concerning Everard and Ariel's descendant, Miranda, and her attempts to come to terms with her family's complicated legacy.

Tad Williams provides an alternative plot for *The Tempest* in 1995's *Caliban's Hour*. The romantic fantasy novel is constructed as Caliban's monologue to a married Miranda, years after the conclusion of *The Tempest*. A deeply wounded and traumatized Caliban ruminates on his betrayal by Prospero and his daughter, revealing how Shakespeare altered and obscured several elements in his version of the story—including how Caliban and Miranda had once been in love and were thwarted from consummating their affections by an interfering Ariel. Caliban also divulges how he, Stephano, and Trinculo attempted to kill Prospero in order to protect Alonso from his vengeance, rather than to gain control of the island. At the end of the novel, having arrived in Italy to confront the now much older Miranda, Caliban must decide whether or not to exact a fatal revenge on his former lover.

Elizabeth Nunez's 2006 novel *Prospero's Daughter* also imagines a romantic relationship between Miranda and Caliban, expanding on the moment in *The Tempest* when Prospero accuses Caliban of "seek[ing] to violate / The honor of my child." On a small island off the coast of Trinidad in the early 1960s, a mixed-race orphan, Carlos Codrington, falls in love with Virginia, the daughter of a white British doctor. In a plot device that mirrors both *The Tempest* as well as the historical colonization of Trinidad by the British, the doctor, Peter Gardner, had seized control of Carlos's mother's house upon his arrival on the island. Gardner, infuriated by the possibility of a romantic union between his daughter and his servant, accuses Carlos of raping Virginia and a British inspector named John Mumsford is called to investigate the charges. As the novel progresses it becomes clear that Gardner—who is not only cruel to Virginia and Carlos but to his female servant Ariana (Ariel) as well—is the true villain of the tale.

Visual Adaptations

Several famous artists, particularly in the eighteenth and nineteenth centuries, have depicted key episodes from *The Tempest*, sometimes reflecting contemporary staging conventions but often imagining scenes implied by but not performed in the play. William Hogarth's take on the play (c. 1735)—arguably the first known depiction of a Shakespearean scene by a British painter—depicts Ferdinand bowing in supplication to a beautiful Miranda, who is seated on a throne and flanked by her stooped, white-haired father and a goblinlike Caliban. The British painter Henry Fuseli's 1789 _Miranda, Prospero, and Caliban_ takes Act One, scene two as its subject, portraying a bearded, barrel-chested Prospero pointing sternly at a scowling, demonic Caliban while an ethereal-looking Miranda stands demurely behind her father. Fuseli also painted a portrait of Ariel (c. 1800–1810), flying on the back of a bat and wielding a whip made of stars; at the bottom of the panel, Ferdinand and Miranda lie locked in a tender embrace.

John Everett Millais and John William Waterhouse, two members of the Pre-Raphaelite brotherhood who produced famous paintings of _Hamlet's_ Ophelia, also painted well-known _Tempest_ portraits. Millais's _Ferdinand Lured by Ariel_ (1849) shows a green, gauze-clad Ariel hovering mischievously in the air and whispering in the ear of a slim, bearded Ferdinand. Waterhouse's _Miranda_ (1916) depicts a moment referred to but not actually portrayed in _The Tempest_. A redheaded Miranda stands on a rocky cliff, her hair whipping about her face as she watches her father's storm wreck the King of Naples's ship off in the distance. Her emotional response to the scene is indicated by the tender way she places her hand above her heart.

Neil Gaiman adapted _The Tempest_ in the final installment of his acclaimed _Sandman_ comic book series (republished in the 1996 collection _The Wake_). In Gaiman's fantastic alternate history, William Shakespeare makes a Faustian bargain with Morpheus, King of Dreams: in return for his son Hamnet and two plays "celebrating dreams," Morpheus will grant Shakespeare a talent for writing unparalleled in human history. In an earlier _Sandman_ issue, Morpheus and his fairy subjects watch a special command performance of the first commissioned play, _A Midsummer Night's Dream_. In this episode, Morpheus comes to collect his second and final payment, _The Tempest_. Gaiman draws on the fact that many readers over the years have associated Prospero's resignation of his powers with Shakespeare's own abdication of his art, and likewise uses _The Tempest_ as an opportunity for his powerful, magisterial hero, Morpheus, to bid a melancholy farewell to his readership.

For Further Reading
by Gordon McMullan

Barker, Francis, and Peter Hulme. "'Nymphs and Reapers Heavily Vanish': The Discursive Con-texts of *The Tempest*." In *Alternative Shakespeares*, edited by John Drakakis. London: Methuen, 1985: 191–205. Reads the play's complexities as the product of its implication in the discourses of Jacobean colonialism, encouraging critics to listen to voices other than that of Prospero, notably that of the usurped Caliban.

Bate, Jonathan. *Shakespeare and Ovid*. Oxford: Clarendon P, 1993. Esp. 239–63. A thorough survey of Shakespeare's engagement with Ovid that includes an account of *The Tempest*, emphasizing the extent to which Shakespeare "collaborated" with Ovid in writing the play, in particular through his reworking of the Medea story.

Berger, Harry, Jr. "Miraculous Harp: A Reading of Shakespeare's *Tempest*." *Shakespeare Studies* 5 (1969): 253–83. An early essay addressing the limitations and problems of Prospero's viewpoint and actions, demonstrating the precariousness of his position and the manipulation required to sustain it.

Brotton, Jerry. "'This Tunis, Sir, Was Carthage': Contesting Colonialism." In *Post-Colonial Shakespeares*, edited by Ania Loomba and Martin Orkin. London: Routledge, 1998: 23–42. One of the first essays to re-emphasize the Mediterranean, as opposed to Caribbean, contexts for *The Tempest*, arguing that the play reflects ambivalence over England's belatedness first of all in establishing trade relations with the Ottoman Empire and only secondly in colonizing westward.

Breight, Curt. "'Treason Doth Never Prosper': *The Tempest* and the Discourse of Treason." *Shakespeare Quarterly* 41 (1990): 1–28. Situates the play within contemporary discourses of treason and notes its participation in the euphemization of official revenge as Prospero reestablishes his political dominance while downplaying his reliance on punishment.

Brown, Paul. "'This Thing of Darkness I Acknowledge Mine': *The Tempest* and the Discourse of Colonialism." In *Political Shakespeare: New Essays in Cultural Materialism*, edited by Jonathan Dollimore and Alan Sinfield. Manchester: Manchester UP, 1985: 48–71. Like Barker and Hulme's article published in the same year, this essay reads *The Tempest* as a colonial text, but with an emphasis in this case not only on the colonization of America but also on the plantation process nearer at hand in Ireland.

Burnett, Mark Thornton. "'Were I in England now': Localizing 'Monsters' in *The Tempest*." In Thorton, *Constructing "Monsters" in Shakespearean Drama and Early Modern Culture*. Basingstoke: Palgrave Macmillan, 2002: 125–53. Argues that *The Tempest*'s discourse of monstrosity paradoxically demonstrates its engagement with

English, rather than colonial, culture and that in this context Prospero himself comes to seem as monstrous as Caliban.

Fuchs, Barbara. "Conquering Islands: Contextualizing *The Tempest.*" *Shakespeare Quarterly* 48 (1997): 45–62. Draws on earlier work to demonstrate that *The Tempest*'s implication in early modern discourses of colonialism extends far wider than simply to the New World—to the plantation of Ireland and to Ottoman imperialism—and shows that each was understood in terms of the other.

Greenblatt, Stephen. "Martial Law in the Land of Cockaigne." In Greenblatt, *Shakespearean Negotiations: The Circulation of Social Energy in Renaissance England.* Oxford: Clarendon Press, 1988: 142–63. Notes the dependence of theatrical pleasure and political power on the manipulation of anxiety, and analyzes *The Tempest* as exemplary of the dramatic process by which dominance is enhanced through controlled unease and power is maintained through the staging of forgiveness.

Hamilton, Donna. *Virgil and "The Tempest": The Politics of Imitation.* Columbus: Ohio State UP, 1990. Argues that in *The Tempest* Shakespeare directly imitates and rewrites the first six books of Virgil's *Aeneid* within the particular context of James I's court.

Hulme, Peter, and William H. Sherman, eds. *"The Tempest" and Its Travels.* London: Reaktion Books, 2000. An invaluable collection of essays covering all aspects of the geography of *The Tempest* and in the process offering a snapshot of the state of play in *Tempest* criticism at the millennium.

Kastan, David Scott. "'The Duke of Milan / And his Brave Son': Old Histories and New in *The Tempest*." In *Shakespeare After Theory*. New York: Routledge, 1999: 183–97. Emphasizes the Mediterranean location of the play in order to break with the orthodoxy of the 1980s that insisted on reading *The Tempest* as essentially "American" in orientation.

Knight, G. Wilson. "The Shakespearian Superman: A Study of *The Tempest*." In *The Crown of Life*: *Essays in the Interpretation of Shakespeare's Final Plays*. London: Oxford UP, 1947: 203–55. A classic of mid-twentieth-century *Tempest* criticism, offering a Nietszchean reading of Prospero as the epitome of Shakespearean heroes, a "god-man" controlling the play, and embodying Shakespeare's alleged late movement "beyond the subjective."

Lindley, David. "Music, Masque, and Meaning in *The Tempest*." In *The Court Masque*, edited by Lindley. Manchester: Manchester UP, 1984: 47–59. Describes the centrality of music to the experience of *The Tempest*, demonstrating the ambivalent influence of the masque on the play and the manipulative function of music in relation both to the characters and the audience.

Marcus, Leah. "The Blue-Eyed Witch." In Marcus, *Unediting the Renaissance: Shakespeare, Marlowe, Milton*. London: Routledge, 1996: 1–37. Demonstrates the ideological nature of commentary notes in editions of Shakespeare by focusing on the description of Sycorax as "blue-eyed" and outlining the ingenious ways editors, unconsciously sustaining Darwinist racial prejudices, have found to avoid attributing what they considered a Northern European eye-color to a North African witch.

Nevo, Ruth. "Subtleties of the Isle: *The Tempest*." In Nevo, *Shakespeare's Other Language*. New York: Methuen, 1987: 130–52. A psychoanalytic interpretation of *The Tempest*, which reads Prospero's project as a fantasy of omnipotence that is made to confront its own discontents—particularly the inescapability of the primitive and the libidinous within the psyche—on the island.

Norbrook, David. "'What Cares These Roarers for the Name of King?': Language and Utopia in *The Tempest*." In *The Politics of Tragicomedy: Shakespeare and After*, edited by Gordon McMullan and Jonathan Hope. London: Routledge, 1992: 21–54. Focuses on the persistent emphasis on visions of freedom and utopian discourse in *The Tempest*, demonstrating the play's engagement with contemporary discourses of political liberty.

Orgel, Stephen. "Prospero's Wife." *Representations* 8 (1985): 1–13. Takes the absence of Prospero's wife as a figure of the more general question of loss and of absence (particularly of women) in *The Tempest*, in which only Prospero's magical manipulations hold off an overall sense of deprivation.

Pitcher, John. "A Theatre of the Future: *The Aeneid* and *The Tempest*." *Essays in Criticism* 34 (1984): 193–215. Summarizes Shakespeare's dependence on Virgil in *The Tempest*, emphasizing the darker elements in the play and the self-consciousness of Shakespeare's fulfillment of Virgil's image of a "theatre of the future" in the early modern appropriation of the classical.

Thompson, Ann. "'Miranda, Where's Your Sister?': Reading Shakespeare's *The Tempest*." In *Feminist Criticism: Theory and Practice*, edited by

Susan Sellers. Hemel Hempstead: Harvester Wheatsheaf, 1991: 45–55. Asks what feminist criticism can do to interpret early modern plays such as *The Tempest* that willfully exclude women characters and notes critics' ways of addressing both Miranda and her absent mother.

Vaughan, Alden T., and Virginia Mason Vaughan. *Shakespeare's Caliban: A Cultural History*. Cambridge: Cambridge UP, 1991. Offers a narrative of the origins and reception of Caliban from Shakespeare's time to the present, demonstrating the character's sustained resonance in theatrical and literary culture.